TAFF VALE PARK
MEMORIES LOST IN TIME

TAFF VALE PARK
MEMORIES LOST IN TIME

by

GARETH HARRIS

First Published in Great Britain
June 2000
by Coalopolis Publishing
9 Cefn Lane,
Glyncoch
Pontypridd CF37 3BP

© Coalopolis Publishing 2000

Printed by:
ProPrint
Riverside Cottage
Great North Road
Stibbington
Peterborough PE8 6LR

British Library Cataloguing-in-publication Data

Front Cover - Professional Cycling at Taff Vale Park 1908

CONTENTS

FOREWORD
BY BRIAN DAVIES,
Curator of the Pontypridd Historical & Cultural Centre

For over a quarter of a century Taff Vale Park was the focal point of sporting and athletic activities in Pontypridd. Its story is the story of a thriving town whose people worked hard and played hard.

Gareth Harris has again given us a book which can be read with enjoyment not only of aficionados of athletics, but by anyone interested in the social history of the valleys. He paints a vivid picture of a community full of life. Taff Vale Park not only hosted athletics events of international repute; there were also regular carnivals, bank holiday sports, soccer matches, circuses, zoos and agricultural shows. In addition to familiar favourites like whippet racing, Pontypridd pioneered trotting, electric hare-coursing and dirt track racing. In this kaleidoscope of activity we can catch tantalising glimpses of wonderful characters - balloonists, a one-legged trick cyclist, and 'midget' boxers. The remarkable individuals who created and sustained Taff Vale Park get the credit they deserve as really significant figures in the town's history.

This narrative which also lets us see the ugly moments, the confusions, the occasional skulduggery, and sadly the dead hand of Council administration, is a tribute to the newspaper reporting in those pioneering days.

This book is a memorable contribution to the social history of Pontypridd, which I am sure will make all who read it look forward to the author's next volume.

Brian Davies
February 2000

INTRODUCTION
BY THE AUTHOR

As a teenager I attended the Coed-y-lan Secondary Modern School at Tyfica Road, Pontypridd. On arriving as a new pupil I was quickly introduced to sport, and in particular, rugby, and was soon drafted at a tender age into the school under-fourteen team. The home, and most of the away games were played at the Taff Vale Park, Treforest, just South of the town. Visible there were the remnants of what must have been a substantial grandstand, and sloping banks that hinted at glorious past. Older residents of the town often talked about speedway and professional soccer on the ground when they were boys, however, there was no comprehensive history written anywhere about what had happened at Taff Vale Park in the past.

At the end of 1998, Mark Newbery, a member of the Pontypridd Junior and Mini Rugby, who had taken out a lease on Taff Vale Park, asked if I knew anything about the ground. I had already written about the beginning of Taff Vale Park in my book about the history of the Pontypridd R.F.C., and I soon found myself doing more research. What unfolded was a remarkable story of a stadium being built by the rugby club, and then improved by an Athletic Syndicate that brought various new sports to the district, and for many years was the centre of sports in the South Wales valley's. At its peak the Taff Vale Park boasted a banked wooden cycle track, a galloway track, a cinder sprint track down the centre of the field, and the only substantial grandstand to be found throughout the valleys. Little wonder then that it proved a mecca for such activities as athletics, rugby (amateur and professional), soccer, boxing, wrestling, cycle racing, speedway, whippet and greyhound racing, trotting and galloway racing; and early in the new century became home to one of the most famous athletic races in the U.K; the Welsh Powderhall Sprint. With such a story untold in the history of Pontypridd, I decided to write this book.

However, the history of Taff Vale Park is so long that it would be impossible to get it all into one book. Therefore this book chronicles the years from its beginning in 1890 until it was purchased by the local council in 1931, and thanks to people like David Williams, Teddy Lewis and John Edward Brooks, who did so much for Taff Vale Park over the years, I have a fascinating story to tell. Events are recorded in chronological order and appear as reported in the Pontypridd and South Wales newspapers of the time. Some reports were confusing, especially those reporting the 'sale' of Taff Vale Park, when in fact organisations had taken out a lease, and who actually owned Taff Vale Park over the early period of this book, is very difficult say, though it is probable that the land was still owned by the original owner James Roberts until his death in March 1917. I hope that you enjoy this book and that it gives a fascinating look into early sport in Pontypridd, as I recall TAFF VALE PARK and the MEMORIES that have been LOST IN TIME.

Gareth Harris

ACKNOWLEDGEMENTS

In my search for information I am extremely grateful for the help of the following people. Mark Newbury and the Pontypridd RFC Junior & Mini Rugby, for giving me the inspiration to begin this book; Mr. John Phillip Brooks and Mr. Harold Lewis, who gave me invaluable information about their grandfathers; Mr. David Davies (Photo of Greyhound Hotel) and Mr. Phillip Marney, Photographer (photo of the author) and Derek G. Lewis photography. I also would like to thank Messrs. Maldwyn Davies, Gareth Lucas; Bill Lougher, and Gwyn Thomas for supplying other photo's; Mrs. Penny Pugh and the staff of the Pontypridd and Cardiff Libraries; Mrs. Ann Cleary and Mr. David Gwyer for their support at the Pontypridd Cultural and Historical Centre, and last but not least, Mr. Brian Davies, the curator of the centre, who supplied me with photographs for this book, while encouraging me to make the most of my limited literary skills.

This book is dedicated to my Mother and Step-Father
Mavis and Ernie Bates

Chapter One 1890 - 1901

The story of Taff Vale Park is a long and interesting one. From a few small fields and slag tips, it would become the premier stadium in the Rhondda Valleys, and equal to most in the principality. Its history began in 1890 when the town rugby team were searching for a field to play upon, and continues today with the mini section of the Pontypridd R.F.C. making the Taff Vale Park their home. This is the story of Taff Vale Park: -

When the Pontypridd (Rugby) Football club reformed in the summer of 1890 their secretary, Edward Llewellin, set about searching for a ground for them to play on. The previous Pontypridd club had played at Ynysangharad, but Edward did not want to rely upon the whim of Mr. Gordon Lenox, the landlord of the Llanover Estate, and so began a search for a new playing field. He contacted Mr. James Roberts, of Forest House, Treforest, a local councillor, and manager of the Forest Iron Works. Mr. Roberts was a keen follower of all sports and leased the land to the rugby club with permission for them to construct a new stadium. However, there was a lot of work to be done before the ground could be used for 'football' as the land was only a few small fields that lay alongside the riverbank, behind which there were waste slag tips from the old iron works. Edward Llewellin also had plans for a grandstand, but whether James Roberts contributed towards this is unknown, indeed, how the club was to pay for it was never disclosed. In September 1890, the Western Mail carried this story about what was being called the 'Taff Vale Ground ': -

'The field, which is snugly enclosed, lies just off the Tramroad at Treforest and has been levelled and titivated at considerable expense. On the Tramroad side of the ground a substantial grandstand has been erected, and Pontypridd can now boast a ground which would not discredit a far more pretentious locality. Close upon £100 has been spent - and well spent - during the last summer on improvements, so that matches can now be played under pleasant conditions, both to players and public. An entrance to the field from the Tramroad has lessened the distance from Pontypridd

by exactly half. Five hundred cartloads of an adjoining tip has been removed to enlarge and level the ground, and this, with the spacious new pavilion, ought to result in a substantial addition to the gate money. Councillor James Roberts, the owner of the ground, has given the club most generous assistance, and thanks to this and the indomitable energy of Mr. Edward Llewellin, the honorary secretary of the rugby club, the public of Pontypridd and the neighbouring towns may soon have to learn to take intelligent and kindly interest in football and athletics in general.'

The First Game At The Taff Vale Grounds

On September 27th 1890, the first official match was played at the Taff Vale Grounds, when Pontypridd defeated Splott Rovers by three tries to one. Then, on November 8th 1890, 2,000 people watched Pontypridd draw with Penygraig, and on March 7th 1891, the famous Cardiff club made their first appearance in the town, when they defeated Pontypridd by two tries and a conversion to nil. The match, on March 7th 1891, was witnessed by a member of the Glamorgan Free Press reporting staff, who gave this account of a big match in these early days in Treforest.: -

'For the capital ground on which the footballer's of Pontypridd do battle with outsiders, the local team have to thank County Councillor James Roberts, who is in thorough sympathy with all healthy athletics having a tendency to benefit the youth of the district. As an infrequent onlooker, I was led by the glamour that somehow invests a struggle between a young Pontypridd team, and a more pretentious and maybe more formidable rival, and in which the very nature of the case excites sympathy for, in the sense, one's own kith and kin, to fall in with the crowds that on Saturday last were wending their way along the Tramroad to the Treforest Football Ground. On arriving at the field an animated sight presented itself. A large assemblage was arranged as to represent the three sides of a rectangle, the space having a goal at each end. We were informed that the gathering was the largest ever present for a football match in Pontypridd. Besides the human fringe of which I have spoken, a considerable number of sightseers were accommodated with seats

and feet protectors in the grandstand. The stand is a decided advantage, since it enables ladies to be present, and provides an almost certain immunity from bronchitic affections to weak and delicate mortals who rather than stand on damp ground for an hour or so, would be constrained to stay away. As player after player passed the stand on the way to the dressing cabin, he was more or less cheered in proportion to the record he held in football playing. The strains of the Treforest Brass Band at a distance, was followed by the band itself, which took up its position in front of the grandstand. Very soon afterwards, the athletes made for the field and took up their stations of play. The Pontypridd lads played gamely, and I should say splendidly, but the weight of mettle was unmistakably against them, and there are, and can be, no two options, that as they were defeated, which was to be expected, they were certainly not disgraced. I am inclined to believe that the Cardiff team made up their minds for an easy victory, instead of which they left the ground at "time" with a respect for their antagonists which is always felt by a generous conqueror who had just fought a foe worthy of his steel. Finally, one important fact I noted during the interval between the first and second halves of the game. The resting contestants restored their exhausted energies not by alcoholic stimulants strange to say, but by absorbing the juice of lemon slices, supplied by Mr. Parry-Thomas, of the Sportsman Hotel. For a game where endurance, energy, and activity are required, this fact is a note in favour of the Rechabites.'

Tragedy At Taff Vale Grounds

The first season of the 'Football' club at their new stadium was marred on March 21st 1891 by the death of 23 year old Pontypridd threequarter, Noah Morgan, who collapsed towards the end of a home game against Llanelly. He was carried unconscious to a shed on the ground, and after Dr. Howard Davies had been called for, the patient was transported to his lodgings in Rhydyfelin. However, on the following day, Sunday, at 7.30 p.m. Noah Morgan died. At the inquest at the Duffryn Arms, Treforest, the following week, a verdict was reached that "the deceased had died from a compression of the brain, caused by a rupture to a blood vessel resulting from a fall." It was stated that two weeks previously Noah Morgan had received a knock on the head in a game on the Taff Vale Grounds against Neath, and had for a while suffered from severe headache, and that the knock to the head against Llanelly had compounded his earlier injury and ultimately proved fatal. Before the start of the 1891-92 season, a local newspaper gave this view of the improvements that had been carried out in the summer of 1891:

' There is a splendid grandstand on the ground and a pavilion for the players. Previous to the initial match of the season, the committee, captain, and secretary, have been actively engaged in improving the ground, and have completely railed the field from goalpost to goalpost. Besides this, extensive alterations have been made to the grandstand to ensure the comfort of the visitors, whilst the level of the field has been properly laid out. With an eye to business, arrangements have been made for enlarging the entrance to the grounds. What stood for an entrance before was replaced by a large gate suitable to pass a large body, including that of the amiable Mrs. Brown, who will not now have further complaint of the egress.'

Lawn Tennis At The Grounds

The summers of these first years must have seen the Taff Vale Grounds fairly quiet, but it apparently was not totally devoid of action, for it appears that there was a Lawn Tennis Club there. Whether this was in the new enclosure, or a little northward towards the town, where the Treforest Lawn Tennis Club played around the turn of the century, is impossible to tell, but as the following report that appeared in the Glamorgan Free Press on July 25th 1891 shows, there WAS a tennis club: 'A cloth was laid on the lawn of the club, at the Taff Vale Grounds, and about fifty members came to tea. A most enjoyable tea was brought about thanks to Mr. and Mrs. James Spickett.'

The First Appearance Of Taff Vale 'Park'

Up to November 1891, the Pontypridd Football Field had been called 'The Taff Vale Grounds', but the Pontypridd Herald of November 14th reported a name change, and wrote: *'The 'A' team were victorious on the Taff Vale Grounds, beg you pardon, honorary secretary Ted Llewellin, I should have said 'PARK'. I had momentarily forgotten that you have taken your flight far, far, above the degenerate terms of 'Ground', and are no longer willing the home of the 'Rhone' lads will ever again be easily denigrated.'*

No Move For Rugby Club

During the summer of 1892, the Pontypridd Football Club and Maritime Colliery team decided to amalgamate. One of the decisions that they had to make was where they were going to play. The local newspapers openly discussed which field would be best, Taff Vale Park (Pontypridd) or the Maesycoed Field (Maritime), and one commented that the comfort of the spectators should be taken into consideration alongside those of the clubs and players. It was pointed out that the entrance to the Taff Vale Park was fairly good, while the access to the Maesycoed field was simply awful, and furthermore, there was no hope of improving it. A meeting was held to try and come to a final decision. However, it got off to a bad start, the building in which it was held had its roof blown off in a high wind, and eventually they moved to the Maritime team headquarters, the Rose and Crown Hotel, Graig. After a long discussion it was resolved that the final decision be left to the representatives of the Welsh Union, and in a subsequent visit to the town, the arbitrators decided that although the Taff Vale Park was not a model ground, it was the least of two evils, and therefore the amalgamated club should play at Treforest.

On December 3rd 1892 Pontypridd had the honour to receive players from different teams to engage in a Welsh Union trial match at Taff Vale Park to select players to take part in the international matches for that season. The event of this important match being played at Pontypridd stamped the town as a fully recognised football town. In the annals of football, the match would always be remembered as one of decided merit, and therein Pontypridd football enthusiasts were given an exhibition of the noble game like they had never witnessed before. Special trains were run from almost every important town in the principality, and consequently a large number of supporters of each player entered the town. Quite an number of visitors came in by the two o' clock trains, and the principal streets were almost blocked. As the time grew near for the commencement of the game, large crowds could be seen wending their way to the scene of battle, the Taff Vale Park. Two teams were selected to decide between for international honours, and were named "Possibles" and "Probables". It was seen that two local lads, Tom Hemsworth and Harry Stead, were selected to play for the "Possibles", a fact that did the town great credit. The ground was very sloppy, and consequently accurate play was almost out of the question. Every part of the field was taken up by an eager crowd of spectators, and the banks and railway around the field were thronged by the enthusiastic crowd.

The Western Mail reported: - *'The attendance was a capital one, £56 being taken on the gate. Considering this match was played on a new and not very convenient to get to ground like Pontypridd, this must be regarded as very encouraging, and should induce the Welsh Union to bring off all trial matches at the grounds of rising or struggling clubs. The game cannot fail to have got a lift in the Pontypridd district owing to this fixture.* The two teams that played in this Trial match were: -

Probables: Back, W. J. Bancroft (Swansea); Threequarters, A. J. Gould (Newport), Pearson and Norman Biggs (both Cardiff), A. N.Other; Halves, H. P. Phillips (Newport), Wat Thomas (Neath); Forwards, A. F. Hill (Cardiff), A. W. Boucher, J. Hannen, W. H. Watts, T. Day (all Newport), F. Hutchinson (Neath), S. Rice (Swansea), W. Phillips (Cardiff Harlequins).

Possibles: Back, T. England (Newport); Threequarters, P. M. Garret (Penarth), E. Thorogood (Swansea), C. Wilding (Cardiff Harlequins), C. S. Coke (Swansea); Halves, R. B. Escott (Cardiff), Ivor Grey (Morriston); Forwards, T. Jones, A. Lewis (Both Cardiff), Harry Stead (Pontypridd), H. J. Daniels (Llanelly), W. Cope (Cardiff), H. A. Harris (Aberavon), Tom Hemsworth (Pontypridd).

Pontypridd RFC at Taff Vale Park 1892

Pyramid Of Gold

At the 1893 A.G.M. of the Pontypridd Football club it was stated that altogether about £300 had been spent on Taff Vale Park, £63-11s-6d during the 1892-93 period, not including the £15 a year to Mr. Roberts for rent. 'Vericus' in the Pontypridd Chronicle commented: -

' It is not known if the football club has the privilege of including a gymnasium amongst the requisites of the club, but it is a thing to be desired, after all, the ground is all well, and should be after the pyramid of gold that has been spent on it.' At the football club A.G.M. in July 1895, the club accounts showed that the rent for Taff Vale Park for the 1894-95 season had now risen to £17-10s-11d and £3-11-0d for a groundsman. £14-19s-11d had been spent on improvement to the ground, while the money taken at the gate amounted to £177-11s-9d. The rent of Taff Vale Park for season 1895-96 was raised to £20.

The Glamorgan Free Press of September 2nd 1895, previewing the new season told of the club's problems with people sneaking into the Taff Vale Park, and wrote: - *'The admission to the practice match will be the modest sum of one penny, put on, no doubt, with the intention of keeping out the youngsters who have not got the modest 'brown ', and who would otherwise swarm the field. The committee intend being very strict this year in making every person who enters the enclosure pay his admission fee, and to prosecute any persons caught 'creeping' in. For this we cannot blame them, as many grown up persons last year, who ought to have known better, were caught sneaking in, and on one occasion twenty of these ardent supporters (?) of the club were compelled to fork out. Had the number that got in last season without paying, paid, it would almost have wiped out the debt.'*

Spectators Cause Problems

The behaviour of the Taff Vale Park crowds was generally good, but on occasion things sometimes got out of hand in the heat of the moment. After a game against Aberavon on March 30th 1895, a local newspaper remarked: -

'The conduct of a few of the spectators was deplorable, and one or two individuals in the grandstand, who ought to know better, would do well, and add to the comfort of true sportsmen, if they pocket their insolent epithets when they next come to the ground.' However, it was not only unsporting words that occurred on the park and sometimes it developed into a mild form of violence. On St. David's Day 1896, there was uproar at Taff Vale Park when Llwynypia were the visitors. The Glamorgan Free Press carried this report written by the Llwynypia correspondent: -

'A most disgusting exhibition of ill feeling, and a cowardly assault, was made by the Pontypridd spectators on one of the Llwynypia players last Saturday. Rough play was said to have been the cause of it, and of course, the home crowd claimed as usual, that the referee was both blind, and partial to Llwynypia. Well done Pontypridd! You have at last shown your true colours. Please say nothing of Ferndale's roughness to your team again, and look at home if you want fair play! An amusing feature of the game was the umpire putting his flag up once when neither the Llwynypia player nor the ball, were anywhere near the touchline. The referee, who was near the touchline, promptly took no notice of such an impudent trick, and Llwynypia were allowed a fine try.'

The match report was very vague, but it appears that the home spectators had become involved when two opposing players had had a 'Physical dispute'. On November 7th 1896, there was more trouble during a game, this time against Neath. The referee was watching the ball being put into the scrum, when his attention was attracted to two players, Collins, the Pontypridd fullback, and Evans, the Neath right-wing, shaping up before each other in preparation for a fight. The referee immediately, and very properly ordered them off the field. They both proceeded towards the grandstand, where the Neath player threatened Collins with a drubbing in the return match. This ultimately led to blows, and a scene of great excitement took place. The crowd came over the enclosing railings, and the referee, officials, and some constables, had to separate the combatants. The referee then had a consultation with the two captains, and in consequence of the high feelings prevailing, it was determined to abandon the match, and declare it a draw. The Glamorgan Free Press commented: -

'It is a disgrace to Welsh football that such a thing should occur on any ground, and especially with teams who occupy such a prominent position in the football world as Pontypridd and Neath. The referee, although very cool all through the affair, was too lax altogether in the early portion of the match. If he had grasped the situation at first, and put all rough play down immediately he saw it, it would have been much better for all concerned. Both men have been reported to the Welsh Football Union.'

First Sports Event

The following summers at Taff Vale Park seem uneventful, and it wasn't until 1897 that the Pontypridd Football Club, who had the use of the ground for every day of the year, thought about using it in the summer for fund raising, though the Lawn Tennis club still played there, but had now changed it's name to the Taff Vale Park Tennis Club. The Glamorgan Free Press of May 1st 1897, carried this report

'The Pontypridd Football Club intend to organise a sports meeting to be held on Whit-Monday at the Taff Vale Park, and on Friday last a meeting was held at the White Hart Hotel to make the arrangements. Nothing much was done, however, beyond appointing deputations to wait upon local tradespeople and others to solicit subscriptions to be offered in the shape of prizes. At present it is undecided whether the sports will be professional or amateur, but the feeling was generally expressed that the foot events, at any rate, should be open to professionals. It seems more than probable that amongst the attractions will be several fire brigade competitions. Undoubtedly a series of these contests would prove highly interesting, and would have the additional advantage, that the competition could be arranged to take place simultaneously with the athletic events. Sergeant Tom Nott, Pontypridd, is in correspondence with the Pontypool, Newport, and other brigades with a view to

inducing them to compete. The foot events would be open to professionals and cycle races will be run under N.C.U. rules. The events decided upon were: 100 Yards Boy's Race; 120 Yards Open Handicap; 440 Yards Open Handicap; One Mile Open Cycle; and Three Mile Open Cycle Races. In addition to those events there will be a Footballers Race, and probably a Fire Brigade Competition. A possibility exists, too, that the Treforest Cycling Club will run off a club race at the same sports. The efforts of the collectors have, up to the present been crowned with success, and hopes are entertained that the value of the whole of the prizes will be subscribed, leaving the gate receipts, less other expenses, as profit to the club. And they are needed, too, just now. The 120 Yards Foot Race ought to attract the cream of the racing talent of Pontypridd, for, in place of the usual £5, £10 is offered to the man who comes first. The prizes for the other places are in like proportion. The first prizes for the two cycling events being £6 each.'

Favoured by fine weather, the day was a capital draw, and between two and three thousand spectators lined the ropes. The Pontypridd town band rendered selections during the day. The event had been organised by Teddy Lewis, a football club member who would soon become a member of the Athletic Syndicate that would lease the Taff Vale Park from James Roberts. The same event the following year was cancelled due to a coal strike, but in 1899 and 1900 the football club staged several sports days. On Whit-Monday 1899, the Pontypridd Football Club held their second Annual Athletic sports on the Taff Vale Park. The ground had been steam rollered on Thursday in order to render it in good condition for cycling. Fortunately the weather turned out fine, with the result that there was a very large gate, and the club in consequence would probably benefit substantially. The entries were fairly numerous, and several exciting finishes were witnessed, particularly in the cycle events, in one of which young Francis scored a sensational win. The events were: 100 Yards Boys Race; 120 Yards Match (two runners) for £10; 120 yards Flat Handicap; One Mile Novice Bicycle; One Mile Open Bicycle; 440 Yards Flat Open Handicap; Three Mile Bicycle Handicap; and Horse Jumping, won by a horse from Treforest called "Dick".

THE PONTYPRIDD FOOTBALL CLUB

... GRAND...
ATHLETIC SPORTS
(Under the Cycling Rules of the N.C.U.)

Whit-Monday, June 7th, 1897
at 1 o'clock

Official Judges

(Foot) Dr. Ivor A. Lewis, Dr. Howard Davies, Councillors. J. E. Spickett, R. L. Phillips, W. Jones Powell, Lionel Lindsay, Esq; Chief Constable, Morgan Lindsay, Esq; M. W. Morgan, Esq; Firbank King, Esq; J. Davies, Esq; Tom Williams Esq; A. J. Gould, Esq; Ack Llewellin, Esq.

(Cycle) W. M. Morris, Esq; D. Williams, Esq; T. S. Judd, Esq; J. G. Morgan, Esq.

Handicappers:

(Foot) The Committee. (Cycle) Mr. J. Griggs, N.C.U.

Starter: Mr. George Ham.

Treasurer:	**Hon Sec:**
Mr. J. E. Brooks	Mr. Gwilym L. Morgan

Percy S. Phillips & McLucas, Observer Office, 77 Taff St, Pontypridd

Taff Vale Park Leased

In the summer of 1900, James Roberts leased the Taff Vale Park to a group of local business men who called themselves 'The Pontypridd Athletic Syndicate', who intended to turn it into a cycle and athletic ground. The twelve shareholders did not make their names public and at the time were unknown, but were: - Mr. John Phillips, Clerk and Cashier of Pwllgwaun Colliery; Mr. Alfred Llewellin, a member of the W.R.U and former Pontypridd R.F.C. captain., David Williams, Greyhound Hotel; Dr. Howard Davies, Chief Health inspector of the local district; Ivor Howells, John Williams, Henry Hubert, Thomas Griffiths, George Barkaway, Steven Barkaway, Francis Barkaway and Albert Amos. Teddy Lewis, though not a share holder, was the syndicate secretary, and most likely the man who suggested professional athletics. Mr. Lewis was so confident of success, that he was invited to take an equal share with the other twelve if they made a loss or a profit. In later years the shareholders became know as 'the twelve apostles of Sport."

Bands Forced to Stay Sober!

The Tenth Annual Brass Band Contest was held at Taff Vale Park for the first time on July 23rd 1900 under the South Wales and Monmouthshire Band Association, but the organisers were a little unhappy because they felt that they had lost scores of pounds on this Monday owing to the fact that they were prohibited from having intoxicants on the ground and thought it very possible that the contest would be held elsewhere the following year. On August 18th 1900 a Cycle and Sports Carnival (Under N.C.U. rules) was held at the T.V. Park in connection with the Treforest Cycling Club. A huge crowd assembled together to witness the events, and the weather being satisfactory, everybody enjoyed themselves. Further professional sports were held at the Taff Vale Park during September, organised by the Athletic Syndicate.

A Dispute Brings Era To An End

The new Athletic Syndicate gave the football club a contract to use Taff Vale Park for the 1900-01 season, but in January 1901 the syndicate began to build a cinder track around the field. The football club were not happy with the changes being made by the syndicate, and in March 1901 relations between the two began to deteriorate when the Mountain Ash team protested before playing an important Glamorgan League fixture that the field was not the proper dimensions, and that cinders and ashes were projecting from the newly formed cycle track that lay partially on the field of play. However, this objection was rejected by the Welsh Union. At the end of the 1900-01 season an argument over the price the syndicate wanted the football club to pay for the repair of a damaged door, and the details about a new contract, brought things to a head, and ended in the club paying the money and moving to play on the People's Park, Mill Street. This is the club's account of these matters: -

The Pontypridd Football Club A.G.M 1901

The Annual Meeting of the Pontypridd Football Club was held at the long room of the White Hart Hotel on Thursday July 25th, 1901. The secretary, Tom Phillips, said that since December they had not been able to charge for entrance to the enclosure at Taff Vale Park owing to the construction of the cycle track. The Rev. D. T. Jones, the chairman of last year's committee said that they had all heard the balance sheet - a balance sheet he considered most satisfactory, in spite of the huge difficulties they had to overcome in trying to encounter that august body who traded under the name of the Pontypridd Athletic Syndicate. He read an agreement signed by one - an agreement which gave to them the ground for season 1900-01. It was dated October 30th 1900, and signed on behalf of the Pontypridd Athletic Syndicate. It allowed the committee the use of Taff Vale Park for the season excepting the 6th, 8th, and 9th of April for the sum of £10, it being understood that the club should when required remove the goal posts, etc.; and in the construction of the cycle track the syndicate would interfere as little as possible with the portion of field required for football, but the syndicate reserved the right to use the field on any date on which football matches had not been arranged to be played. It was signed by Mr. Ack Llewellin. Continuing, Mr. Jones said that last season the club had rented the field at a rental of £10 per annum. The £10 had been paid and the syndicate had promised them that they would interfere as little as possible with the football field when constructing the cycle track. However, he believed that they could not have interfered more than they had. They had deprived them of one match and not satisfied with that they had made a bill which if paid would go to the flourishing coffers of the syndicate. The speaker then referred to the unique syndicate who were not true sportsmen or they would not do their best to destroy football; they had said that they would not make it a secret syndicate, but would let everyone who wished to, join. However, they HAD made it absolutely private and secret, and the result was that the football club now had to face danger and calamity. He did not believe that they could use the Taff Vale Park again because those gentlemen had taken the park into their own hands and spoiled it as far as football was concerned. He was positive of one thing, if football was played on the Taff Vale Park it would be nothing but a source of trouble. The committee had decided if possible to steer clear of the syndicate by getting another field. The South Wales Daily News of September 16th 1901, summed up the situation that had arisen between the 'Football' club and the Pontypridd Athletic Syndicate like this: -

'Since the close of last season circumstances arose which culminated a short time ago in very unpleasant relations to prevail between the club and the local athletic syndicate which has leased Taff Vale Park, and which has been the rendezvous of footballers for many years. A cycle track has been laid there, and as the two clubs could not agree on terms whereby the ground could be used for football, matters came to such an impasse that the football club committee threw up the sponge in absolute disgust, and secured the Mill Field, also known as the People's Park, for the coming season. This is greatly deplored by all true lovers of sport and without entering into the merits or demerits of the dispute, one is forced to admit that it could have easily been decided to the satisfaction of all concerned had both parties shown a little more conciliatory spirit, and not kept their "Backs Up" so stiffly. The result is that the Taff Vale Park, the scene of many exciting contests and one admirably suited for the game, is temporarily closed for it, and one can only hope that

football and the fortunes of the team will not suffer on the new ground, which is the only one available in the town.'

Athletics Thrive

1901 saw Taff Vale Park being fully used in the summer for the first time, and was used for several weekends and bank holidays from May until September for Sports and Athletics meetings, organised by the Athletic Syndicate. The Pontypridd Observer of July 13th 1901 gave this forecast of one such meeting: -

'Everything points to a very successful Sports and Cycle Meeting at the Taff Vale Park on Monday and Wednesday next. The chief interest is centred on the fifty guinea challenge bowl, presented by Mr. Dewar, M.P; for which all the well-known cracks of England have entered. There are also record entries for the other events, including Rowland, Johnson, Polytechnic Cycle Club, London; Sidney Hill, London; Allen, and several other well-known athletes from Bristol and the West of England; Griggs, Metcalfe, Prickett, and others from Cardiff, will also put in an appearance. Such a great event should be a draw, and we trust the crowd will crowd the Taff Vale Park next week.'

The Athletic Syndicate Committee held a meeting on Tuesday, August 27th 1901 and approved the application of the Graig schools for a loan of the Taff Vale Park for tea and sports. A long discussion took place as to whether professional sports should be held and it was explained that the National Cycling Union had suspended the cycle tracks where which held unregistered meetings. It was felt that by doing so the N.C.U. were not legislating in the interest of cycling in general. It was decided that the N.C.U. should be asked to rescind their resolution, and allow professional cycling on one day and amateur on another, and a deputation consisting of Mr. David Williams, Mr. Ack Llewellin and Mr. Ivor Howells was appointed to wait on the South Wales Centre. Several applications to hold professional matches on the Taff Vale Park were refused, it being explained the N.C.U. would not grant permits.

Graig School Sports

The Graig Schools Sports Day on Friday, September 21st 1901, seems to be the first school sports to be held on the Taff Vale Park, but would become the first of hundreds over the decades. The children had on an excellent treat in the form of racing, games, etc., which had been arranged for them by Mr. J. W. John, manager of the schools. The park, kindly lent by the athletic syndicate, presented a picturesque appearance when the children assembled. A well arranged programme had been prepared, which consisted of 24 events, which included: Girls 50 Yards Handicap; 50 Yards Girls Skipping Handicap; 50 and 60 Yards Girls Handicap's; a Three-legged Race, and a 440 Yards Boys Handicap. The prizes numbered about 120, several being costly articles, and were distributed to the winners by Mrs. W. Spickett. Buns and tarts were provided by Mr. Chubb, and afterwards the children dispersed hoping that such an event would become an annual affair. The children of the lower standards each received a small present with sweets and fruit.

End Of The First Ten Years

On January 1st 1901, the construction of a track at the Taff Pale Park had commenced, and the first sports held on Easter Monday. Eleven sports meetings, plus cycle matches were held that summer. Sports were now seen in Pontypridd that had never been seen before in South Wales. The new era at Taff Vale Park had started well, the rugby club was gone by September, but how long would the Athletic Syndicate adventure last, and how much success would they achieve? Only time would tell!

Chapter Two 1902 - 05

1902 saw eleven sports and various other events organised by the Athletic Syndicate, and an exciting summer saw Pigeon Shooting, Whippet Racing, Foot Racing, Cycling, and a Parachute Jump that went very wrong. But the major event was the formation of an Athletic club at a Pontypridd Central Cycling Club meeting in March, when anyone who was interested were asked to attend.

Whippet Racing Cheats At The Taff Vale Park

'Idris' in the Glamorgan Free Press of April 5th 1902, gave this report about the Easter programme at the Taff Vale Park: -

The sport-loving public in Pontypridd and district have during the festive weekend been catered for in quite a lavish style. On the Taff Vale Park we have had pigeon shooting, whippet racing, amateur and professional foot and cycle events. The promotion of the above attractions evidently meant the getting of the nimble sixpence in some fashion or other. The pigeon shooting competition drew a strong entry list, but was not much patronised by spectators. Of those present watching the starting proceedings, few seemed to understand how the competition was decided. Each man had one shot. If he killed he moved into the second round, but if he missed he was out of the competition altogether. Round after round went on in this way until ultimately only three were left. The first prize was annexed by Mr. Llewellyn Hughes Jnr; Llantwit, the second by Mr. Evan Morgan, Trebanog, and the third by Mr. Richards of Newtown.

On Good-Friday afternoon whippet racing was the attraction. This form of sport drew a much larger crown than the shooting. Some very good racing was seen, but the majority of the heat winners had a soft thing on. This is the first time anything of this kind has been attempted in South Wales. Next time we have this sport the promoters would undoubtedly know more about it, and we should see closer finishes in the heats. A rather amusing story is going the rounds in connection with a very well known Pontypridd sportsman. Before Friday's events came off he was asked what he though whippet racing would be like. He informed the speaker that there was one good thing about it, and that was that once the dogs were slipped there could be no faking. Cycle riders and foot runners can cut it up and select as they like, but in whippet racing everything was straight and above board. The sportsman referred to, will not have such an excellent opinion of dog racing in the future, I think. The way in which some of the dogs were started, or rather, hindered in starting, was disgraceful. There were two events, one the local and one the open. The veriest novice easily perceived that the open event could be comfortably won by a little dog from Lancaster called Jack, who was not much bigger than a fair sized cat. His owner, when the pistol went for the final, held him for a good second, thus losing him about 15 yards, and then, instead of slipping him straight, threw him across the track. A great many believe that even then he would have won had he not collided with a bitch called "Rose", and been thrown and badly hurt. The winner of this event was a dog called "Miss Nauton", Rose coming second. The local race was won by Mr. Ille's "Jack", "Prince Illife" was second; and Mr. McKenzie's third. There was some grumbling in this because Jack was said to have been a Bristol dog, not a local one. It was rough luck on Mr. Jim McKenzie, the footballer, in this race. His dog and his bitch won their heats comfortably, but were pitted against each other in the semi-final. Some other arrangements ought certainly to have been made.'

A record crowd attended at the Taff Vale Park on Monday afternoon, when Professional Foot and Cycle Racing was announced. Some capital racing was seen, particularly with Barden, Syd Jenkins, and W. Rees of Llantrisant. A very handsome "Glamorgan Free Press Challenge Cup" was won by Syd Jenkins, of Cardiff, last years English champion. There were two motor cycle races in the programme, but they did not come off. There were three motors on the ground, but two of them would not act. The third, ridden by an American named Rogers, was set going for the edification of the spectators. He completed a mile in one minute and forty-nine seconds. He could have done it in a faster time, but did not like one part of the track. He had been accustomed to circular tracks, and did not feel at home on the park. The spectators were afterwards put into a very good humour by the antics of Barden, the champion cyclist, who mounted a motor cycle, and endeavoured to emulate the American, Rogers, but could not get the speed out of it.

Whitsun 1902

It was not a crowd, but a multitude, which assembled on Monday afternoon, May 19th 1902, to partake of the handsome annual Whitsun feast provided by the Pontypridd Athletic Syndicate. Pontypridd was accredited by some to be slow in moving, but the success and increasing popularity of meetings at the Taff Vale Park is a direct negative so far as sport is concerned, and reflected the highest credit upon the foresight, judgement, and generosity of the committee responsible for the arrangements. With the large concourse of people and great number of events competed for, culminating with the daring flight from the crowds by Miss Viola Spencer at an altitude of between four to five thousand feet, not a single hitch occurred to mar the enjoyment. Several other lady parachutists had offered their services, but in order that everything should pass off artistically, the Pontypridd Athletic Club engaged Miss Spencer at a very much larger sum than the others demanded. In reference to the parachute performance, much speculation was rife during the afternoon as to whether Miss Spencer would make the ascent. The wind had been boisterous in the night, and did not modify except at short intervals throughout the day, and notwithstanding the risk, the daring young lady decided to essay her perilous task, and, fortunately, with complete success. At about 8 o'clock expectancy was at its height, and not only in the enclosed grounds, but at the Common and all the neighbouring hillsides all heads were raised skyward as the balloon shot up in the air, and headed towards Llantrisant. Up! up! up! until the eye was strained to the utmost tension to see the brave woman at all. One's heart for a moment seemed to stop beating, as from a dizzy height, like a bolt from the blue, the break away was made, and the frail Aeronaut floating in space gracefully descended amidst the re-echoing cheers of thousands who had witnessed the brilliant parachute display. On Tuesday another large gathering took place, the events being confined to professionals. Miss Spencer again made another successful parachute descent.

Last Rugby Club Athletics Day

Despite the Pontypridd Football Club having moved out of Taff Vale Park, they still held a sports on the Park on Friday May 23rd, 1902, no doubt thanks to Dr. Howard Davies, a Taff Vale Park Shareholder, and president of the rugby club. However, it seems that the local public were keeping their money for the sports the following day when the Athletic Syndicate had arranged a good programme, for the Football event only attracted a small attendance, and £20 was lost on the day. Because of this it was the final Annual sports day the rugby club held.

In a meeting of the Athletic Syndicate on July 21st 1903, a brave decision was made when it was decided that they would hold a £100 sprint.

The August Bank Holiday 1902

The Pontypridd Athletic Club continued their bank holiday sports meetings at the T.V. Park when a programme confined to professionals was held on Tuesday, August 6th 1902. There was a large number of entries - over 200 - of which 50 were in the 200 Yards Sprint, 64 in 120 Yards Sprint, and 30 in the 120 Yards Flat Handicap (Local). The fact that Charlie Barden, the world's ex-champion cyclist, would attack Tom Linton's one hour cinder track record - 30 miles- 650 yards - made on the T.V. Park track on June 26th (Coronation Thursday) 1902, also created a large amount of speculation. It was 5.30 p.m. when Barden started his attempt, and was paced by a motor. He covered the first mile in two seconds less than Linton, but lost it in the second mile. He continued at a good pace, but in the second lap of the ninth mile his effort was brought to an end, owing to a tendon in his right leg being sprained. Shortly before this the motor machine misfired and Barden shot past, only again to be overtaken by the motor. It was jumping to get behind the motor machine that his misfortune happened, and at that time his record for eight miles was 15 min. 54 secs. as compared with Linton's 15 min. 10 secs. The park was crowded to its utmost capacity when Miss Viola Spencer, London, made her balloon ascent. The balloon with the solitary passenger, ascended to a height of about 7,000 feet, and subsequently glided towards the Common. Miss Spencer and her parachute landed a few yards away from the Rocking Stone. The balloon came to earth near Mrs. Bassett's house near the Common. September 8th 1902 saw another successful athletics meeting held at T.V. Park. The events and entries were numerous, including the five mile amateur Welsh cycling championship. On Thursday, October 16th 1902 a sports day was held at Taff Vale Park in aid of the Pontypridd Free Library. The Tug of War, 8 a-side, was very keenly contested, not withstanding the heavy downpour of rain which took place during the competition. the winning teams were: - 1, Abergorki; 2. Cilfynydd. Several choruses and test pieces were rendered by the Hopkinstown Male Voice Party under the conductorship of Mr. Evan Howells. These were also given in the rain. The fireworks were not let off as it was too wet.

1903

International Cycling Racing At Pontypridd

In 1903 the Pontypridd Athletic Syndicate opened their season on Monday April 13th. There was a good attendance and the day's programme consisted of professional foot racing and cycle events. The Pontypridd Volunteer Band was in attendance.

One of the most interesting cycle meetings ever promoted in South Wales was that held at the Taff Vale Park on Saturday May 9th 1903. Six celebrated continental riders came over to this country for the express purpose of competing against the best men who were riding as professionals under the auspices of the S.Wales Centre of National Cyclists Union. Councillor David Williams had used his influence to bring about the meeting, which was held to celebrate the reaffiliation of the National Cycling Union to the Union Cyclist International. Chief amongst the visitors was Piard, who was considered one of the finest riders in Paris. Another famous cyclist was Grogna, of Belgium, and the other four were Meyer, Germany; Conelli, Italy; Meller, Austria, and Domaine, France. Tom James, Tonypandy, was the most conspicuous figure amongst the Welsh professionals. It was seen that the continental drivers captured nearly

Undated photo of T.V. Park with wooden cycle track looking North

all the prize money, and their riding it must be said, was greatly superior to that of the local men. The only grievance of the visitors was the rule which attains on the continent of the riders in the race waiting for an opponent when he has punctured his tyre, was not acted upon at Pontypridd. It has never been the custom to do this in this country.

Disturbing Events At Whitsun 1903

The highlight of the 1903 Whitsun Athletics Meeting at the Taff Vale Park for many people was the proposed parachute jump. However, it did not go as planned. The Glamorgan Free Press the following week, gave this report:

'The Ynysangharad field was the scene of a serious accident on Whit-Monday afternoon. Captain A. E. Smith, of the firm of Spencer & Co., London, was engaged to give a performance at the Taff Vale Park sports, and made the ascent with his wife, who is known as the "Countess S". The event was watched by thousands of people on the Common and the hillsides near the park. Both persons sat side by side in the balloon, which shot into the air without the slightest hitch. It was about 5 o'clock, and there was no wind to interfere with the proceedings. The balloon, therefore, went up in an almost perpendicular direction. The parachutists were on opposite sides of the balloon. About a couple of minutes after the balloon had left the ground the countess was seen to drop, and when the parachute expanded the crowd cheered lustily. The Capt. followed, and the cheering was renewed. It was soon seen, however, that the descent of the performers was not going to be accomplished without difficulty and the two parachutists drifted up the valley to Ynysangharad and came down within fifty yards of each other. The lady became entangled in the branches of a tree, and Capt. Smith got hung up on the telegraph wires, which pass over the River Taff at the point where he descended. The greatest excitement prevailed, and a large crowd soon collected. The countess sat in the tree quite unconcerned until a ladder was brought from the chainworks, and by means of this she came to earth again. Taken away in a cab, when asked if she was hurt, replied, "No, Thanks. I feel all right

now, and I am glad to get down." Capt. Smith was in a much worse plight, and he was for a considerable time clinging to the telegraph wires. He asked a fireman to go for a fire-escape, but was informed that it was impossible to take it into the water. He was offered the jumping sheet, but refused to take advantage of this. He proceeded to unfasten his apparatus from the wires and dropped into the water. Some amusement was caused by his falling onto the heads of a number of men who were in the river anxious to render him assistance. The momentary humour was, however, quickly turned to what seemed like a tragedy. It was stated that it had been the intention of the captain to work his way along the telegram wires to the nearest pole, and thus make his descent, but as the crowd were leaving, the wire on which he was standing gave way, and he fell like a log into the river, which at this point is very shallow. As he fell his nose came into contact with a wire, causing him a serious wound, and it was seen that his face was covered with blood, and he was taken in a half-fainting condition to a cab which was waiting. Dr. Evans, who had been playing tennis at an adjoining field, at once took the injured man to the County Hotel, where he had been staying, and Dr. Morgan Rees was also called in. It was discovered that the Captain had sustained severe injuries, which consisted of a fracture of the girdle of bones on the lower part of the body, and a serious rupture. His condition was considered so serious that it was decided to remove him to the Cardiff Infirmary. He was taken to Cardiff by the evening train to the institute. The second ascent, which was arranged for Tuesday was abandoned, Mr. Spencer, who was performing at Pwllelli, being unable to reach Pontypridd before 8 o'clock in the evening. Smith's employers - Messrs Spencer Bros. - wired on Tuesday afternoon from London: "Much grieved here at the accident; suggest subscription, to which we will subscribe." We are authorized to state by the chairman of the Athletic Committee, Councillor David Williams, that the pair will not suffer any loss by not going up on Tuesday, but will be paid as if the ascent had been made."

PONTYPRIDD
TAFF VALE PARK
WHIT MONDAY AND TUESDAY 1902

The best way to spend your holidays is at the Taff Vale Park to see the acknowledged:-

CHAMPION LADY PARACHUTIST OF THE WORLD,

ENGAGED AT ENORMOUS EXPENSE FOR BOTH DAYS.

ALSO THE FIRST APPEARANCE OF TOM DAVIES, MANCHESTER, EX-AMATEUR CHAMPION, AND NOW A CYCLIST IN THE WORLD OF PROFESSIONALISM

ALSO GASCOIGNE AND BARDEN THE CHAMPION CYCLISTS AND RECORD HOLDERS, RECENTLY RETURNED FROM A TOUR IN GERMANY, SPAIN, FRANCE ETC.; EDMUNDS, BRISTOL; PRICKETT, CARDIFF; JENKINS, PONTYPRIDD; REES, LLANTRISANT; D. J. EVANS, SWANSEA

A MATCH WILL ALSO TAKE PLACE BETWEEN MESSRS JONES AND MAY FROM YNYSYBWL THE BEST OF TWO OUT OF THREE PURSUIT. RACES FOR A GOLD WATCH ON MONDAY.

IN ADDITION TO LARGE PROGRAMMES, AN EXCELLENT BAND HAS BEEN MADE FOR THE GREAT CROWD EXPECTED

AN ATTEMPT WILL BE MADE TO BREAK THE ONE-MILE RECORD FOR MOTOR CYCLE BY AN AMERICAN CHAMPION.

Admission ONLY 6d. Enclosure and Grand Stand Extra

G. F. Press May 17th 1902

August Bank Holiday 1903

On August 3rd and 4th 1903, the sports at the Taff Vale Park drew an immense crowd, and again demonstrated the good done to the ratepayers by the enterprising Athletic Syndicate. The attractive programme of two days sports opened on Monday, with the result that the entries were the most classy ever seen on these grounds. The events were confined to amateurs, who included Duffy, America, the World's Champion Sprinter and 100 yards record holder; Reginald Wadsley, the Mile Champion; Brevill, 200 Yards English Champion; A. Norton, Midland Counties 100 Yards Champion; and crack cyclists, including Benyon, Wrexham; A. L. Reed, of London; and Brooks of London. Some exciting and interesting racing was seen, especially in the cycling events, and the gate was a record one.

The second days sports took place on Tuesday afternoon, and the attendance was a good one. In the morning driving drizzling rain swept over the town, but by the afternoon had ceased, and the weather was all that could be expected. Tuesdays events were confined to professionals, and included: M. Williams, America; White, Elswick; Thomas, Lasswade; Struth, Edinburgh; Cook, Helenburgh; Broad, Manchester; Jones and Lewis, Wolverhampton; Ferguson, Dundee; and D. Thomas and Harrison, the Welsh cracks; Syd Jenkins, the English Cycling Champion, who carried off three firsts at Carmarthen the week before; Bert Howard and Tom Williams also took part. Big prizes were offered, and principal amongst the events was the Twenty Mile Motor Paced Race, for which a £20 prize was offered. A condition of the race was that the distance be covered in 60 minutes, otherwise the judges would declare no race.

As a result of the One Mile Paced Race at the August Bank Holiday, in which Barkway secured a splendid victory, a re-match took place on Saturday, September 5th 1903, between Barkway and Rees. The race was of ten miles, behind motor pace, wind shields being allowed. Rees, after the seventh mile, got away and secured a lead of a lap, but unfortunately his racing machine got out of order and left the track. Barkway now secured a lead of two laps, and from now

27

until the fifteenth mile Rees was differently paced by various riders, only one of whom was fast enough for him, viz; Jack Sheen, Aberdare. At the fifteen mile he was again paced by his former machine, and succeeded in lapping his opponent. He was, however, unable to make up the lost ground, and was beaten by a lap. Barkway, who rode very well, was paced by Joe Evans on a 4 h.p. Yennard motor. Rees was paced admirably by Harry Prickett, and, but for the accident to the motor, it was thought Rees would have won with a substantial lead.

Athletic Club Take The Lead

The Glamorgan Free Press of September 12th 1903, reported:

'It would appear that the Pontypridd Athletic Club is taking the lead throughout the kingdom in the way of sports. The Yorkshire "Tykes" would hardly have credited the "Gallant little Wales" with the pluck to offer the plum prize of the sprinting world, yet such is the case, and it will be contested on Saturday at the T. V. Park. The first prize of £80 is well worth the winning, and many and special advantages are offered to those who compete, no really good man on the track, as a matter of fact, need go away empty handed. Mr. T. E. Lewis, who is acting as handicapper, has given general satisfaction in his handicapping, and the name of Councillor David Williams, as referee ensures fair play to all that may enter.'

Dispute At First 'Powderhall' Sprint

On September 14th 1903 a Sports and Athletic Meeting was held at Taff Vale Park, and was later considered by the Pontypridd Athletic Club to be the first of the Powderhall races. However, this time the professional handicap sprint, with prize money of £80 for the winner, was called "The Welsh Sheffield Handicap". There had been 60 entry forms filled in, but only 40 were accepted, and 10x4 runner heats were run. The Glamorgan Free Press the following week gave this report: -

'A singular development has arisen out of the Welsh £100 Sprint at Pontypridd this Monday last, and one which may have curious results. It appears that a formal objection has been lodged by W. L.

Sherwood, formerly of Leigh, but now of Bridgend, against Harry Howden, of Edinburgh, who was first home in the sprint and won the £80 prize, on the ground that Howden was the assumed name of a well-known pedestrian capable of doing a better from his mark of 13 yards, than done at Pontypridd. We understand that no allegation has been made as far as his last three performances go, but that the entry form was not correct. In the meantime the prize money has not been paid over to Howden. As against his objection it may be stated that Joe White, of Elswick, asserts that Howden is the same Harry Howden that he has competed against in other events, and that he is well known to one North-Country sprinter who has been running of late in Wales. Until enquiries are made bets and prizes are withheld, but what may happen should Howden be disqualified is not certain.'

When spoken to the following Wednesday Mr. Ted Lewis, secretary of the Athletic Club, stated that the objection came as a great surprise to him. The winner of the handicap went through all the formalities and fulfilled the conditions laid down. He had entered as Howden, and, unless proved to be another man, would be paid as Howden. Joe White, said that he had run against Howden three times at Hawick that year, and at two other places which he could not remember. He had also run against him in the Powderhall Sports (Scotland) on several occasions, and he had not the slightest doubt as to his identity. Charles Payne, the official handicapper, said there was no doubt as to the winner of the handicap being Howden. This was stated publicly after the race in the smokeroom of a local hotel in the presence of members of the Athletic Committee. It may be mentioned that White won the £100 handicap at Newcastle. Quite a feature of the meeting was the manner in which Mr. Ted Lewis got his men away. In almost every instance they seemed to rise exactly together, and this by their actions endorsing the grand opinion of Mr. Lewis expressed by Mr. Manning, Half Mile Champion of England, who stated that Ted was one of the fairest and best starters in the country. Duffy was the only man who has beaten the pistol at the Taff Vale Park sports, but accomplished his purpose in the final, and won himself a big bottle of wine, he having backed himself to beat the starter.

"Veteran" also commented: - *'As is usually the case, when a man gets through an exceptionally fine performance, conjectures are rife as to whether Howden was a "Dark Horse" or not. Scotchmen say that he has never done anything of noteworthy on the track before, and his entry form showed no prizes in his last three attempts. Some athletes in order to win a coveted prize run for a long time simply for a mark. The Merthyr boys are credited with bringing him down from Edinburgh. They know a thing or two Penydarren way! Such a huge gate assembled to witness the finals on Monday, that I suppose we can take it for granted now that a big handicap will be an annual affair. It is certain the Pontypridd Athletic Club drew in a much bigger revenue than the whole amount of the prizes they distributed. Good luck to them! It had been felt for the last twenty years that a first class cycle and sprint track were required, but no-one seemed to have the courage to do the necessary. Hence the Pontypridd Athletic Club must be commended for their enterprise and initiative they have exhibited during the time the club has been in existence.'*
The result of the first 'Welsh Powderhall Sprint' was - 1. Harry Howden, Edinburgh, off 13 Yards; 2. W. I. Sherwood, Bridgend, 12½ Yards; 3. W. H. Harrison, Cardiff, 10 Yards; Joe White, Elswick, 6½ Yards.

Cycling At Pontypridd - Tom Linton v Tom James

On September 21st 1903 the cycling season closed with a match for a £50 aside between Tom Linton and Tom James, but was marred by a chapter of incidents. In the first place Linton's pacer, from Paris, lost himself on the railway, having left London at 7 a.m. that morning, and did not arrive at Pontypridd until the 6 p.m. train. Three races were to be run, 3, 5 and 10 miles. In the three mile race J. R. Evans attempted to pace Linton, but it was soon seen that Linton had no chance of winning. For the second race of five miles Linton was paced by a motor and beat James. At the end of the second race Linton's pacer arrived, and much humour was caused as he tried to instruct his pacer in French. After five miles, Linton had lapped the Mountain Ash Champion, but soon after James had the misfortune to buckle his front wheel and retired from the track.

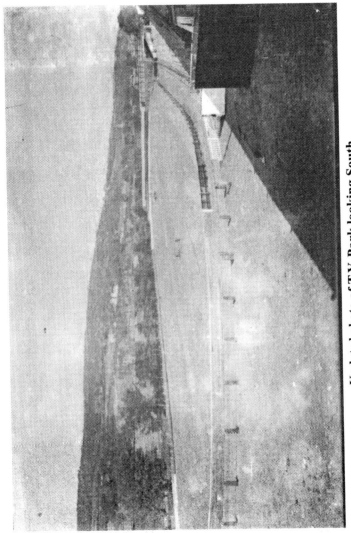

Undated photo of T.V. Park looking South

Linton and his pacer ran out the ten miles in fine style, increasing speed at the finish, amidst resounding cheers from the crowd.

On October 10th 1903, the local newspaper, the Glamorgan Free Press, gave this interesting interview with a member of the Athletic Syndicate,: -

The revival of athletic sports at Pontypridd during the last three years has been hailed with the liveliest satisfaction by the sportsmen throughout the country. The old prestige of Pontypridd had gone, and it seemed that the athletic feeling was dead amongst the rising generation. This has proved to be an error; it has not yet died, but lay dormant; it remained for such giants as Mr. David Williams, Greyhound Hotel, and what have been facetiously termed "The Twelve Apostles of Sport" to put their hands together and awake their slumbering disciples. It was a difficult task, and the monetary risk was great, but it was decided to make a track at the Taff Vale Park, do everything on the best possible scale, give good prizes, act fair and straight in every particular, and sink or swim by endeavour. They have given the time and energy ungrudgingly, and no one in South Wales, or wherever racing men are found, will begrudge the syndicate (now called the athletic club) the success it has achieved and so richly merited. The head and front of the whole thing has been Mr. David Williams, and a representative called upon him to obtain a few particulars as to the rise and progress of the club, and was received with studied courtesy, and given the following interesting particulars:

"The construction of the track was commenced on January 1st 1901, and the first sport was held there on Easter Monday following. Eleven sports meetings, besides cycle matches, being the record for that season. In the year 1902 we had eleven sports and special meetings, and let the track gratis to the N.C.U. to hold championship races. This year we only held seven meetings, owing to the competition getting keener, but I should think it would be the best year for athletes in the history of the sport in Wales. Successful sports being given all over the country, we attribute the result to the way the club conducts its business in Pontypridd. The discipline exercised over all the athletes, the support given to the club by the public, and to the untiring efforts of the secretary, Mr. Ted Lewis, may be attributed the success of our three years working. As you know, our secretary is now acknowledged as the handicapper (Professional) for Wales, and all sport promoting bodies, who are anxious for good finishes, and every athlete to run all the way to win, are wise to engage his services. There are many quite capable of doing good handicapping, but you must be up-to-date, and watch the performances of every athlete to give a good result, and this knowledge is well within the grasp of Mr. Lewis.

You must understand that the Amateur Athletic Association and the National Cyclist Union have adopted the system of one handicapper only for a very wide area for many years. They hold annual meetings with their respective unions, and all the officials are elected then, and a fee is charged for any event in the handicap, so that during the existence of the official handicapper, any fast runner in sprint handicaps knows within a yard his mark, and the cyclist within, say 5 yards. Of course, there are scales of penalties printed on every programme, which further assists the amateurs, so that he invariably knows his mark before he gets his programme. The club has followed this system with the professional contests, and to learn how the professionals appreciate our good intention all you have to do is see our entry list. I believe, said Mr. Williams, in this respect we hold the record. For many events we give big prizes, the best prize given years ago (perhaps with an occasional big prize) was about £5. Now £8 and £10 are given in many places. We have the best possible talent of sport on our ground, the champions in both foot and cycling. Say, for instance, Pease, the Irish champion, in my opinion, the best cycling sprinter I have ever seen; Reed, the present champion, Benyon, Wills, Jansen, Ingram, and several other in amateur sports. In professional, we have had Chinn, Jenkins, Gascoyne, Piara, Meyer, in fact, as I have told you more than once, the cream of the athletic world have appeared. As regards to the sprint track, it is the opinion of such champions as Duffy, Downes, Wadsley, Morton and several others, the finest sprint track in the United Kingdom. It is perfectly level, 30 foot wide, 530 feet long, and although only recently made, the surface is in very good condition, and we hope that by next season the surface will be perfect. Our grandstand, of course, is not finished as it should be, but as it is, is very serviceable, and we can guarantee it to be strong enough to hold all that can possibly cram together on it. The seating capacity is for two hundred. I should like to fix a row of seats on the river side, the same as there are on the enclosure end, but we are compelled to leave the road without obstruction. We should like to see the ground protected better by larger trees, as we have such a very large and appreciative crowd of spectators on the Newport - Caerphilly railway embankment and surrounding hills, who seem to thoroughly enjoy themselves at the cost of others. I am, however, pleased to say that we have some excellent supporters who are always prepared to pay the admission price, knowing full well that they will get the worth of their money. We are very well supported by strangers, and, by the way, I should like to draw your attention to this fact that since our ground opened we consider that we have brought thousands to the town, who otherwise would have gone to Cardiff and elsewhere, and of course, have been the means of providing our natives with sufficient inducement to remain at home, because, as I have mentioned before, we provide the best talent, and if you were to journey to the Crystal Palace you could not see a finer show.

Our dressing rooms for competitors are considered good by all athletes. We have the lounge and shower bath and other conveniences under the same roof, there being also plenty of room for the rubbing down process on the Parisian massage system, a professional masseuse being on the premises where you can guarantee to get fit and well for all severe contests in fourteen days. The ratepayers of the town have certainly benefited. And I may tell you that the club has received the thanks of several tradesmen in the town for the additional trade they consider they do whenever the club hold sports on the Taff Vale Park. In fact, there were many restaurants in town who had to close early on September 14th, having completely sold out. Then there is the Taff Vale Railway Co. - it must have been an additional receipt to their passenger account; the same thing applies to Cabs, Brakes Ect. Besides, there is the Cycle Agent, Boot and shoe dealer, Hosier, in fact, there are several trades who must reap considerable benefit. Again there is the police force, the payment of constables to ensure order is a very big item. I could not say off hand, but I should think we have paid some scores of pounds to the county for police services. Then there are the printers, who must benefit by the grounds, and the National Cycle Union, who receive 10/6d for permission to hold amateur or professional sports, and in the event of an amateur of professional cycling meeting taking place at the same sports, we must pay the sum of £2-1s; also 10/6d for every match at the ground. Of course the funds of the local centre of the N.C.U. have swelled considerable since our assistance, but, (like Cardiff) no credit is given to Pontypridd.

It was in January last that the first member was appointed to represent the valleys on the executive council, of whom there are nine representing South Wales and Monmouthshire, and that member has an important motion to come on at the annual meeting. Then we are considered of such importance that we must be included amongst the taxpayers. Why? I don't know. With the rental heavy, swelled by rates and taxes, the club is dealt with a very heavy hand indeed. Since the visit of one of our members to Paris this summer, where he saw paced racing at its perfection, the committee has decided to accede to that members request and will hold in the first place a 10 Mile Paced Race, with £20 first prize, and £10 second, with £2 expenses to unplaced riders in the final, with the result that the paced racing can fit in, and will be an important factor in the future sports. I consider I was the happiest man on the track on Saturday last when Billy Rees, after winning his match with Barkway (one of the best seen on the track) continued for the hour, and did practically 34 miles in that hour, a truly remarkable performance. It is considered by some that Billy can do better. I told him last June that he could do 35 miles in an hour, but he and others thought it impossible. However, taking into consideration the drawback with the pacing machine, he would have fulfilled my prediction. Unfortunately for Rees his performance will not be recognised, because he had no official timekeeper on the ground. The fee of timekeeper is an addition to other fees, hence the reason of one not being present. I am pleased that it is over for this season.

There is a great deal of worry and anxiety in connection with it, to get everything in apple-pie order. All spectators are your critics, and you must not have many mistakes, or you hear of it. I assure you that I feel quite run out. But excuse me, I have a meeting, and I must be off - Good day, thanks for calling."

It had been an exciting year for the Athletic Syndicate. They had formed themselves into the Pontypridd Athletic Club, and brought into it sports loving enthusiasts in the town who had not become shareholders, but were nevertheless influential in local sports. The introduction of the '£100 Welsh Sprint ' was a major step forward. It appears that Mr. Ted Lewis and one or two others had travelled up to Scotland to watch the Scottish Powderhall races, that were held over the new year period, and recommend to the Syndicate that they offer the largest prize ever offered in Wales. It was a huge gamble, but had proved a success, and would be a major event for several decades. The Pontypridd Cycle Club was also formed this season, hence people reported before as 'riding out' of Mardy etc; were now reported as being from Pontypridd.

Easter 1904

On Easter Monday and Tuesday, 4th and 5th April 1904, a most extensive programme had been arranged for the holidays, and the best of the talent available had been secured. There were 33 entries for the walking competition, which was a record for such an event in Wales, and in the foot events the champions of England, Scotland and Wales competed. The cycling events also brought out some of the fastest sprinters in England and Wales, and altogether the number of entries totalled 300. There could be no hesitation in saying that these sports proved to be the finest in the principality over the Easter Holidays, and the promoters deserved the large support of the pleasure seekers and sport loving public of the district generally for bring in such a host of talent. The highlight of the two days was the 120 Yards Handicap, which would in later years be regarded as the second of the Powderhall races. More than 500 people turn up for the £100 Welsh Sprint, as it was advertised. There were three heats, and in the first, Joe White, Elswick, off 7 yards, beat the favourite, Fred Lewis, Hopkinstown, the Pontypridd Football Club wing-threequarter, off 16 yards, by six inches. After a false start, Fred Coombes, Penygraig got away and won the final by half a yard from Joe White.

Final result: - 1. Fred Coombes, Tonypandy, 12½ Yards; 2. Joe White, Elswick, 7 Yards; 4. A. T. Jenkins, Bedlinog, 18 Yards; 4. Dan Evans, Tonypandy, 16 Yards.

Whitsun 1904

More profession sports were held on June 11th 1904 at T.V.Park. There was a Half Mile Professional Scratch Cycle Race; Ten Mile Profession Scratch Cycle Race; and a One Mile Novice Cycle Handicap. In final of the latter, six competitors, while taking the last lap, came in contact with each other, and three riders came off, but were not seriously injured. The motor cycle race between Tom Williams, Hafod and Barkway, Mardy, for £50 aside, was abandoned owing to the rain. Two weeks later, on June 25th 1904, a Twelve Mile Motor Paced Race for £10 was run off on a Saturday evening between Tom Williams and E. Barkway. An unfortunate accident took place when Williams and Barkway and his pacer, were thrown from their machines, and both sustained injuries which delayed the race for nearly an hour. It was restarted just after 7 o'clock.

August Bank Holiday 1904

A sports and athletic meeting held on July 31st and August 2nd 1904 by the Pontypridd Athletic Club, was favoured by splendid weather, and there was a big attendance. The chief item of the day was the appearance of Duffy, the American flyer, and Morton, London, his vanquisher at Rochdale a few weeks before. They competed in the 100 yard event, both being at scratch. They were, however, were knocked out in their respective heats, Duffy in the first and Morton in the last, though they had left their marks well, and went away in grand style, gaining considerably upon the winners who had a start of 12 and 12½ Yards respectively. Duffy was beaten by about 1½ Yards and Morton by a little more. The final was not reported. Other events and winners were: A One Mile Scratch Cycle Race, won

TAFF VALE PARK, PONTYPRIDD

GRAND AMATEUR & PROFESSIONAL
ATHLETIC MEETING
ON EASTER MONDAY, APRIL 4TH, 1904.
CYCLE EVENTS (Amateur and Professional) under
N.C.U. Rules

PROGRAMME OF EVENTS
FOOT
1. - 100 Yards FLAT HANDICAP (for boys under 15 years)
2. -.120 Yards FLAT HANDICAP (open)
3. -. 300 Yards FLAT HANDICAP (open)

PROFESSIONAL CYCLING
5. - ONE MILE SCRATCH
6. - Half mile HANDICAP (open)
7. - One mile HANDICAP (for novices)

AMATEUR CYCLING
8. - Half mile HANDICAP (for novices)
9. - One mile HANDICAP (Open)
10. - ONE MILE SCRATCH

Handicappers: Foot, TED LEWIS, Pontypridd. Cycle Events Mr. R.
J. B. Rind, Cardiff.

See Small Bills and Posters for the Great Monster
BRASS BANDS CONTEST.

C. Maynon, Cardiff; 100 Yards Flat Handicap, T. Mclean, Cardiff; One Mile scratch Cycle Race for the Graig Brewery Cup, E. Handley, Pontypridd; One Mile Scratch Cycle for the Worthington Shield, W. Edmunds, Bristol; and various other events.

On Tuesday, more professional sports were held at the Taff Vale Park. Some of the results and winners included: 120 Yards Flat Open Handicap, H. John, Rhydyfelin; One Mile Cycle Race, D. J. Hughes, Cwmavon; One Lap Hurdle Handicap, S. Page, Abercynon. Five Mile Scratch Cycle Profession Championship of the N.C.U. South Wales Centre, Tom Jones, Mountain Ash; Two Mile Walking Handicap, W. Williams, Merthyr; Five Mile Motor Paced Race, E. Barway, Bath (paced by Evans, Treforest).

Welsh Powderhall 1904

The Welsh £100 sprint, 1st prize £80; 2nd, £8; 3rd, £3; 4th, £1, attracted over 5,000 spectators to the Taff Vale Park on Saturday, September 3rd 1904, and the good gate cheered the promoters who deserved financial success, the sport was of high quality, and the spectators were delighted, particularly over the results of the sprint, which produced a grand contest, and gave victory to a middle-marker who had been running consistently well during the season, and had secured about fifteen firsts. Fred Coombes, of Penygraig, the winner, had a reputation as a straight runner, and his win was due to his pluck, which enabled to do the running in the final heats, while more fancied men on Saturday lost their form by Monday, this being notably the case with Fred Lewis, of Hopkinstown, who was an even favourite before the first heat of the semi-final, though he had beaten the veteran Joe White of Elswick in his heat, he was not able to do so on Monday, when he had two more yards. The winner's running and the survivors of the preliminary heats was a tribute to the scrupulous fairness of the handicapper. The final itself was a great struggle. All got away well after a false start through misfiring of Teddy Lewis's pistol, and Coombes ran gamely and won by half a yard, a yard dividing second and third, with fourth just behind. Result 1904 Welsh Powderhall: 1st Fred Coombes, 12½ Yds,

Tonypandy; 2nd, Joe White,7 Yds Elswick; 3rd A. T. Jenkins, 18 Yds, Bedlinog; 4th Dan Evans, 16 Yds, Tonypandy.

The other big event was the 25 Mile Professional Cycle Championship Race. The prizes were a gold medal for the winner and silver medals to riders beating the time standard of 70 minutes. A limit of 80 minutes was fixed. Early on J. Williams, Pontypridd, was lapped, and retired, while E. Jones, Boncath, had a puncture. The 20 miles was covered in 55 minutes, but were not going fast enough to get much. Tom Williams of Hafod, looked the good thing the betting showed him to be, when Tom Lewis, Ammanford and H. Rees, Pentre, came croppers. Lewis lost a lap before he could remount, and then sprinting probably saved the others from exceeding the standard time. It was a great race in the last lap, Burgess, Porth, riding well, but was outsprinted by Tom Williams and George Breen, Pontypridd, a popular win being gained by Williams by a length, with Breen second and Burgess third.

1905
Easter 1905

The 1905 athletic season was opened on Easter Monday, April 24th 1905 with amateur cycling and foot events, and various events were heavily contested, especially so in the finals. The weather was fine and a good crowd present. There were four unfortunate incidents in the cycle events, but fortunately none met with serious injuries When the third heat of the One-mile novice handicap was being run, one of the men fell when rounding the bottom bend, and B. Evans, Treforest, who was following directly behind, was unable to avoid him, and was pitched clean over the boards protecting the track. The mishaps were due entirely to careless driving, a number of competitors committing the fatal mistake of looking behind them when going at top speed, thus losing control of the machine. A keen fight was made for the Graig Brewery Challenge Cup, a One Mile Scratch Cycle Handicap, won by J. Voyce, Pontypridd.

On Tuesday professional cycle and foot events were held. A thick, drizzling rain fell during the greater portion of the day, and the poor weather adversely affected the attendance, which was very meagre.

In the morning in was contemplated postponing the sports, and a meeting of the committee was called. It was admitted that even with a moderate gate a loss from £40 to £50 would be sustained if the programme was carried out, but in the interests of athletes and cyclists, many of whom had journeyed a long distance, and to avoid disappointment, the committee resolved not to abandon the event. Although the track was heavy, the races were completed in fast time, and some exceptionally keen competitions were witnessed in both the heats and the finals. The outstanding feature of the day was the fine riding of Syd Jenkins, Cardiff, in the One Mile Scratch, which he won easily, and in the Quarter Mile Handicap. In the latter event he had to give a good start, but he won amid great cheers. Lisk's, Penygraig, effort in securing the 120 Yards Handicap was an excellent one, and he showed great pluck when it seemed odds on the limit man getting home first, and just won on the tape. The One Mile Scratch Race for the Glamorgan Free Press' Challenge Cup proved good sports, and in the final there was an exciting finish. All four kept close together until they reached the final bend, when Flint, who was leading, made a spurt, Syd Jenkins, however, soon forged ahead, and maintaining the lead won by a length and a half from James. Result: 1st Syd Jenkins, Cardiff; 2nd Tom James, Mountain Ash; 3rd Tom Williams, Trehafod. The most exciting race of the day was the Quarter Mile Cycle Handicap. Syd Jenkins, Cardiff, who was on scratch, accomplished a splendid feat in winning his heat, the limit man being 40 Yds on. In the final he was left a hard task, but the Welsh champion rode well, and on the first straight picked up speedily. Coming round the final bend he was a few yards behind Churchill, but ten yards from home he overtook him and won by half a length. There was also a 100 Yards Footballer Handicap, won by W. E. Blacker, Penrhiwceiber. The following day there was a band contest.

Whitsun 1905

June 12th and 13th 1905 saw athletic sports at the Taff Vale Park. On Monday excellent amateur sports were held. Rain fell at intervals, and this affected the attendance. The Quarter and One Mile Championships of the N.C.U. were won easily by C. E. Baker,

Carmarthen, who was the hot favourite. In the 120 Yards flat sprint, four men breasted the tape almost in a bunch, and the judges were set a difficult task in allotting them their respective positions. The introduction of a Two Mile Cycle "Devil Take the Hindmost" was especially an attraction owing to the rules - the last man in every lap was to be withdrawn - going for all they were worth, and it was probably the fastest long cycle race that had taken place on the park. This event was won by E. Handley, Pontypridd. On Whit-Tuesday excellent professional sports were held under the auspices of the Pontypridd Athletic Club. There was a good attendance, and though rain fell heavily during the morning, it cleared off before the commencement of the sports. On July 1st 1905, a Brass Band Competition took place at the Taff Vale Park.

August Bank Holiday 1905

There was a large attendance on the Taff Vale Park on August bank holiday Monday, August 9th 1905. There were several cycle events including a Half Mile Cycle Handicap; One Mile Novice Cycle Handicap; One Mile Cycle Handicap, and One Mile Scratch Cycle Race. The main cycle events, however, were the Half Mile Cycle Championship of the South Wales Centre, N.C.U; - A good race resulting in C. Baker, Carmarthen, getting home a wheel in front of E. Handley, Pontypridd, and the Five Mile Handicap, also won by Baker. The five men kept together well until the final lap, when Baker forged ahead and won easily. A popular event was the One-lap Boys Obstacle Race, and as the boys passed through ladders, under tarpaulins, and through barrels, roars of laughter were evoked, and the winner of the first heat was greeted with prolonged applause. The second heat was less exciting, but the final was watched with the liveliest of interest, and was won by J. Reardon, Pontypridd.

During the afternoon the local Volunteer Band rendered selections of music. At the close of racing, C. G. Stevens, who was described as the "Daredevil Barber of Ferndale" ascended in one of Spencer's balloons. There was little wind and the sky overhead was quite clear. The balloon shot up almost perpendicularly. Stephens smiled as he left the ground, and twice waved his hand, the last time when he was almost out of sight. There was breathless excitement as he released his parachute and descended without a hitch. Later in the evening there was dancing on the green, and a display of fireworks. On Tuesday, the professionals competed in cycle and track events.

Welsh Powderhall 1905

At the Taff Vale Park on September 2nd 1905, chief interest centred on the £100 130 Yards foot Handicap, the Welsh Powderhall, in which the entries would be unusually large, amongst others being Struth, Edinburgh; Harry Howden, Edinburgh; B. George, Lanark; B. Day, Blackpool; T. Jones, Carmarthen; G. Baily, Salford; and all the cracks of South Wales. The first prize was £80, with £8, and £3 respectively for second and third, and £1-10s each to the winners of the heats who did not get a prize. Excitement ran high as the twelve heats were run off and a great deal of money changed hands in the betting enclosure. After the four semi-finals, the final was contested by Lisk, Penygraig; and Bailey, Graham and M'Clean, Cardiff; though Bailey was thought to have the best chance. When the pistol went M'Clean seemed to lose a bit at the start. As a consequence of this, Graham practically led from the outset, and when the half distance had been covered it was seen that the issue lay between the latter and Bailey. The Salford man made a tremendous effort, but just failed to reach Graham, by a rare inch or two. Bailey disputed the ruling of the judge, Mr. David Williams, and for some time it seemed there would be a rumpus, as the Salford man had many backers, and people crowded inside the course. Mr. Williams firmly adhered to his decision, however, and was supported a by Mr. Tom Williams, who timed the run off. The final result of the 1905 Welsh Powderhall was: -

1. A. J. Graham, Cardiff, 12½ Yards; 2. G. Bailey, Cardiff, 5½ Yards; 3. P. C. Lisk, Penygraig, 8½ Yards; 4. T. M'Clean, Cardiff, 11 Yards.

The day had started with the final of the 25 Mile Scratch Cycle Handicap championship for the South Wales Centre of the N.C.U. Ten started, but only four kept on the track until the bell rung, when a fine finish was witnessed, and saw Churchill winning the £12 first prize. Other events on the programme were the heats of the One Mile Cycle Handicap, which saw a dispute in the fourth and last heat, when one competitor, Churchill, fell, breaking his machine, and accused Tom James of boring and lodged an objection that was turned down; and a 880 Yards Foot Handicap, with a first prize of £12, won by F. C. Davies, Tenby; while the 300 Yards Foot Handicap was won by W. Reardon, Pontypridd. Another profession sports meeting was held on Monday September 10th 1905, under the auspices of the South Wales Racing Syndicate. The main event was an International Cycle Race which was won by Reynolds, Ireland; with Chinn, England; and Tom Williams, Wales; second and third respectively.

The Athletic Syndicate had during these first three years built up a good following at Taff Vale Park, cycling being in the predominance, but the £100 130 Yard Handicap Sprint, the Powderhall, was steadily growing in stature, and beginning to attract many overseas athletes. Would this continue in the second part of this decade, or would the sporting spectators of the district become bored with it all?

Chapter Three 1906 - 10
Rugby Club Return To T. V. Park

1906 saw weekly sports meetings and the bigger annual events at Easter, Whitsun and August bank holidays continue, but the major change this year would be the return of the rugby club to T.V. Park.

The 1906 A.G.M. of the Pontypridd Football Club at the White Hart Hotel on July 23rd was a torrid affair and the outcome of it all saw the throwing over of the old officials and committee, and as a consequence, Mr. Gregory, the manager of the chainworks, refused to lease the Ynysangharad field to the club maintaining that the committee and officials were not constitutionally elected and that persons who were not bona-fide members of the club were allowed to freely participate in the voting. Negotiations were subsequently successfully carried on to secure the Taff Vale Park and happily for the club supporters, the Athletic Syndicate placed the park at their disposal. However, several of the players strongly objected to playing on Taff Vale Park, alleging unsuitability owing to the cinder track running down the centre of the field, and the nearness of the asphalt track to the touchline. Therefore, with a view to obtaining the old ground at Ynysangharad a deputation waited upon the newly elected committee to endeavour to persuade them to call a meeting of members and prospective members. The upshot was that the idea of a members meeting was rejected. People were asking if Ted Lewis or Ack Llewellin, members of the Athletic Club, and the Welsh Union, could be asked to arbitrate on the points at issue before the position was further aggravated. Mr. Llewellin, however, was convinced that the Taff Vale Park was not suitable to play football on, and two days later the ground difficulty was brought to the attention of the W.R.U; but no definite resolution was passed. On September 5th 1906, the Pontypridd Football Club held a trial match at Taff Vale Park. The cinder track down the centre of the field was covered with a preparation of sand and bark to the depth of a few inches. Though it cut up badly when played upon, it was contended by the officials that with a little rain it would effectually set. Several players when interviewed expressed themselves thoroughly satisfied - in fact enamoured with the success of the preparation of sand and bark. *"It does not interfere with the play at all"* said winger Freddy Lewis *"and is not as heavy going as you would imagine. When I scored the last try I scarcely felt any difference running over it than on the turfed portion of the field."* A few days later a sub-committee of the Welsh Union visited Taff Vale Park and decided the field was suitable for play, and so for the 1906-07 season the Pontypridd Football Club were back on Taff Vale Park.

The Welsh Powderhall 1906

The 1906 Welsh Powderhall took place on Saturday, the 2nd and Monday 4th of September, when there was again reportedly a record attendance. The main event was the 130 Yards Foot Handicap, first prize £80; second £8; third £2; fourth £1 with 10/- each to the winner of the heats. On Saturday there were 16 heats run, and after the semi-finals on Monday the four finalists were W. A. Rees, Port Talbot, 13 Yards; W. T. Davies, Blackwood, 8 Yds; T. Adams, Swindon, 12 Yards; and D. Christopher, Edinburgh, 5 Yds. The sprint final was the last event of the meeting and intense excitement prevailed during the twenty minute interval before it began. Each man as he went to his place on the track received encouraging applause from his supporters. The race was a "chest contest", Christopher winning a magnificent race. Davies was second, Rees third, and Adams fourth. Christopher was 5ft-9in in height and was 28 years of age. He was well known in South Wales, having in 1902 won no less than 22 first prizes in Welsh meetings. It was estimated in 1906 that he had over the years won over £4,000 on the track. In the final of the Five Mile Scratch Cycle Race for the professional championship of the South Wales Centre and N.C.U. gold medal, thirteen started and the men kept together until the last two laps. Churchill of Penygraig's, machine broke down, and he lost a lap while a new bicycle was found for him, but, pulling up in fine style, he won by a wheel from Syd Jenkins, Cardiff.

1907

Easter Monday 1907 saw Taff Vale Park the rendezvous of a characteristically big crowd to witness the amateur sports. All the competitions were keen, and in nearly every instance, the finishes were very close. The Whippet Racing took a unique place in the programme, inasmuch as it was a recent innovation in the sports, and no less than forty dogs were slipped. The first prize was won by G. Mathias, Llantwit, with "Dorothy", in an interesting race.

On May 20th 1907, the Athletic Sports and Military Tournament at the Taff Vale Park established a record. There was a magnificent programme of amateur events which drew in a huge crowd, and was without question the finest day's sport ever put before the South Wales public. It was an amateur's day, and the entries were a superbly representative lot. The military tournament was an innovation, and was most enthusiastically welcomed by the gathering. It was a picturesque display, and was a big success. In addition to the cavalry contests, a first rate Gymnastic Display was given by the talented corps under the direction of Sergeant - Instructors Roulet and Cambell. As well as the military tournament, there were also tent pegging and a Lemon Slicing Contest (on horseback). The cycling races were especially well contested. The blue ribbon event was the One Mile Scratch Cycle Race for the "Worthington Shield ". Edmunds, Bristol, had to win on this occasion to secure the shield as his absolute property. He was, however, successfully challenged by George Summers, London.

August Bank Holiday Sports 1907

Ideal weather favoured the band contests at T.V. Park on August 4th, 1907 - Bank Holiday Monday. There was, however, a rather disappointing attendance. Chief interest in the contests, which were held under the rules of the South Wales and Monmouthshire Brass Band Association., was centred in the competition for Messrs. Bass and Co.'s 100 Guinea Challenge Shield, which carried with it a cash prize of £30. The Ferndale Prize Band, who were previous holders of the valuable trophy, were again successful. Ten bands entered this contest, but only three took the field. The Ferndale Band afterwards discoursed sweet music at the promenade concert at Ynysangharad. In class "B", the Dinas Band was adjudged the winner, but Mr. W. Breeze, the president, on behalf of the Band Association, lodged an objection on the grounds that one player had played two instruments

TAFF VALE PARK PONTYPRIDD

WHIT MONDAY & TUESDAY, MAY 20TH AND 21ST 1907

GRAND MILITARY TOURNAMENT AND ATHLETIC SPORTS

WHIT-MONDAY - Great Military Tournament and Display, by Crack Cavalry men of the 9th and 17th Lancers, 7th Hussars, 4th and 7th Dragoon Guards, and a selection on Infantrymen.
CAVALRY - Heads and Posts, Cleaving Turks' Heads, Lemon Cutting, Tent Pegging, Etc. Etc. INFANTRY - Military Marching, Free Gymnastics, Vaulting Horse, Horizontal Bar, Pyramids, etc. Military Clowns.

AMATEUR ATHLETIC & CYCLE SPORTS

WHIT-TUESDAY

GREAT PROFESSIONAL ATHLETIC AND CYCLE MEETING

Magnificent Entries- SIX COUNTRIES WILL BE REPRESENTED BY THEIR CHAMPION CYCLISTS:-

FRANCE, PIARD; AUSTRALIA, HELLER; AMERICA, GERMAIN; ENGLAND, J. S. BENYON; A. A L WHILES, W. B. CASEY, + GEORGE FLINT, LONDON; WALES, SYD JENKINS; IRELAND, HARRY REYNOLDS.

Admission (each Day) one shilling. Children under 12 in charge of parents, Free. Gates open 12.30 p.m.; Sports commence 2 p.m. sharp

The Best Athletic Meetings in Wales.

- the euphonium and the trombone, but this appears to have been over ruled.

Welsh Powderhall 1907

The victory of Charlie Evans, Tenby, in the final of the Welsh Powderhall of 1907 was probably one of the most popular that had been known since the initiation of the handicap at the Rhondda metropolis. There was a ton of money on him, as may be gleaned from the fact that he started at the extra-ordinary price of 3 to 1 on. Moreover, it was not the money of his backers that brought him to so hot a favourite, but rather that of the general public, who were on him to a man. After winning his heat so decisively in the first round, it was suggested that Evans could find another two yards if necessary. That in itself, was a remarkable tall order. That considerable credence must have been given to the rumour was evident to the fact that at the opening of the wagering on Monday morning he was a sound even-money chance, and the fielders were not by any means anxious to take wagers to any extent at that price. From somewhere or other Evans found a good time in his heat in the second round, and in beating a so red-hot a favourite as Lewis, of Rushton, it was no wonder that odds were immediately asked for about his chances in the final. Evans always had the opposition well beaten. He seemed to be held by T. Taylor and Thomas, up to three parts of the journey, but after that he came out full of running, and simply romped home by a yard and a half. Davies, was disappointing, for after going well for over half the journey he seemed to die away. Taylor ran prominently, and there were many who thought that he had finished closer to the winner than the official verdict made him out to be.

Final Result 1907 Welsh Powderhall: 1st, Charlie Evans, Tenby, 10 Yds; 2nd, D. E. Thomas, Treforest, 13 Yds; 3rd, W. T. Davies, Blackwood, 5½ Yds; 4th, T. Taylor, Cardiff, 11 Yds.

Rugby Club Abandon Taff Vale Park

Around Christmas 1907 the town was rife with rumours of a professional Rugby team being formed in Pontypridd by several ex-members of the amateur club, and that they were intent on getting the field at Ynysangharad. The Daily News around that time gave a little history of what had happened in the town: -

'The crystalising of the movement for a Northern Union club at Pontypridd has given rise to a discussion as to the primary reason underlying the project. The promoters were at one time keen supporters of the amateur club, and considerable dissatisfaction was aroused two years ago when the committee decided to change the venue of the playing field from Ynysangharad to the Taff Vale Park. It was predicted at that time that the takings would diminish, as the Taff Vale Park was far removed from the centre of population. The anticipated result has, unfortunately for the exchequer of the amateur club, been fulfilled. Not only did the change effect the attendance, but several of the players held a deep rooted objection to the new ground. In fact, this was the immediate cause of Duncan McGregor, the ex-captain and Scottish international, severing his connection with the team, and other defections can be directly traced to the same cause. The old field, Ynysangharad, situated in the centre of town, was at the disposal of the committee this year, and its rejection - or to be strictly accurate, the indisposition of the committee to approach the landlord to secure it - caused further dissatisfaction. At least this was the chief reason given by one of the prime movers in the present venture when questioned. And the assertion is further supported by the fact that the new club is bent on securing the old field at Ynysangharad. If they succeeded - and they are very sanguine on the point - then the professional club would command better patronage than a team who plays their matches in a place removed from the populous centre.'

A well attended meeting of the proposed professional Northern Union rugby club at the Maltsters Arms on January 24th 1908, appears to have forced the Pontypridd Amateur club to rethink their policy of playing at Taff Vale Park and rushed them into leaving, and the club must have at last approached Mr. Gregory about the use of the Ynysangharad field, for at the start of February 1908, the club was back at Ynysangharad. Whether the amateur club returning to Ynysangharad had any effect on the plans for a professional club, who thought Taff Vale Park was too far from the town centre, it is hard to say, but the plan for a Northern Union team disappeared after this date.

1908

The Pontypridd Athletic Club committee were to be complemented on an excellent and lengthy programme offered for the 1908 Easter meeting at the Taff Vale Grounds. The weather, on both Monday and Tuesday, was decidedly wintry, but not withstanding this the programme, which included several new features, attracted about 2,500 persons on Monday and 2,000 on Tuesday. The One Mile Walking Handicap, was won by E. J. Kelly, Pontypridd, off 160 Yards, and the 150 Yards Whippet Handicap, was won by Ted Vaughan's "Monkey."

There were thirteen entries in the 9 Stone Wrestling Contest, Thomas Jenkins, Pentre, and F. Wright, Cardiff, being the finalists. The final bout lasted 43 minutes. Wright continually attacked, and the referee, Councillor Wright, ultimately gave the combatants the Cumberland lock, and Wright was declared the winner amidst the plaudits of the crowd. In the 10 Stone Amateur Wrestling Competition, Charley Thomas, Newport, threw E. G. Jones in one minute 30 seconds, and was, therefore, declared the winner.

Considerable amusement was caused by the wrestling on Easter Tuesday, April 20th 1908, For this there were four entries - W. Randall of Bridgend, Robert Hillman of Porth, and Edgar C. Powell and Arthur Martin, both of Pontypridd. Powell was disqualified for being too heavy, and Watkins, of Treforest, took his place. The initial bout between Watkins and Martin caused a lot of fun, as Watkins, although he constantly got his opponent on his back, could not get his two shoulders on the ground at the same time, Martin continually rolling away and avoiding defeat, but eventually Watkins succeeded, in 28 minutes. The second bout, between Hillman and Randall, did not afford much sport, as it only lasted three minutes, Hillman proving the victor. In the final, Hillman at once threw Watkins with such comparative ease, in less than a minute, that the referee doubted the sincerity of the wrestlers, and ordered them to the mat for a second time, at the same time warning them that unless they displayed earnestness he would disqualify them. The warning had a good result, as the men were pretty well matched, and after six minutes Hillman proved the victor.

Glyntaff Fete And Carnival

The First Annual Fete and Carnival in connection with the Glyntaff parish church and schools was held at the Taff Vale Park on Saturday July 17th 1908. The first part of the programme was a grand procession, in which a large number of persons took part. Assembling at the Glyntaff Schools, and headed by the Albion Colliery Workmen's Prize Silver Band, the procession wended its way along Pentrebach Road, Bassett Street, Middle Street, Taff Street, Wood Road, Park Street, and the Tramroad to Taff Vale Park. Prizes were offered for the Best Tradesmen's Turn-out, the Best Dressed Donkey, Best Decorated Cycle, Best Comic Dress, and Best Dressed Boy or Girl. The sports included a Five Mile Motor Cycle Race; and a Five Mile Motor Cycle and Ordinary Cycle Race, in which J. Evans, who rode an ordinary bicycle was passed by the single cylinder motor bike which carried a wind shield, ridden by K. Bryant, by almost a mile. During the afternoon a squad of schoolboys from Glyntaff School gave an exceedingly good gymnastic display.

August Bank Holiday 1908

The Pontypridd Athletic Club were once again highly commended on the success of the professional sports at Taff Vale Park on August 4th 1908. The club had a good name for promoting excellent meetings, and the attendance was exceedingly satisfactory. There were no less than 250 different competitors. The feature of the programme was the galaxy of pedestrians, the entrants for the 120 Yards Open Handicap numbering 118, and those for the novice totalling 68. This indicated a revival in pedestrianism in Wales, and amongst the runners, all of whom were on the youthful side, there were several who showed promise of making really first class men, and the finishes were particularly keen. Bert Morgan, who was two years before fancied for the Welsh Powderhall brought off a popular win by inches in the 120 Yards Open Handicap, and Randall, Bridgend, finished strongly in the 300 Yards Handicap. The most brilliant performance of the day was that of F. C. Davies, Tenby, who was rapidly coming to the front as a record sprinter, who won the Half Mile from six yards behind scratch, in a remarkably good time. He ran magnificently and reached the tape a yard in front of Hodgson. T. Harvey, Rhydyfelen, who was beaten by half a wheel in the quarter mile, gained an easy victory in the half mile, after riding grandly. In the 120 Yards Boy's Handicap Stan Morris, age 7, ran exceedingly well and gave good promise of making a good athlete.

The Welsh Powderhall 1908

This meeting that began on Saturday Sept 7th 1908, was reportedly the best of the September meetings since their inception in 1903. The public attendance was large, due to the grand gathering of crack sprinters who had entered for the chief event. The first event of the day on Saturday was a One-Mile Scratch Cycle Race for the Professional Championship of the South Wales Centre, N.C.U; which was won by D. Hughes, Brynaman. James, who passed the post first, being disqualified for "boring." For the main event, the 130 Yards Foot Handicap there were 90 entries. It was run in 16 preliminary heats on Saturday, the final being reserved for Monday's programme. The majority of the heats were very closely contested. Day's success in winning his heat was the signal for loud applause. The next event was a Half Mile Foot Handicap in which first prize was £20, Second, £4; and Third £1. There were 58 entries. The two scratch men, B. R. Day, Blackpool, and F. C. Davies, Tenby, did not turn out and evidently reserved themselves for the final of the big sprint on Monday. Todd, the Australian, was also a non-starter for the same reason.

There were four semi-final heats for the big sprint on Monday. In the first heat the favourite was Day, and he fully justified expectations when he defeated F. C. Davies, 13½ Yards; Tom Meredith, Cardiff, 12 Yards; and B.Morgan, Penrhiwceiber, 15½ Yards. It had been a splendid start, the four men getting away with the crack of Ted Lewis's pistol. All eyes were concentrated on Day, and he gained gradually upon his opponents. When he had travelled 100 yards he got abreast of Davies, and leaving nothing to chance, went bang up to the tape at full tilt, winning by 1½ Yards. The other three who made the final were Thomas, Pontymoel, 12½ Yards; T. Adams, Swindon; and Rees of Glanaman, 13½ Yards, who had beaten Postle, Australia, who pulled up because of an injured thigh. In the final a splendid start was made, and as Day gained inch by inch the spectators could hardly contain themselves. R. O. Rees, however, seriously challenged him, and after running the last ten yards neck and neck, Day won by inches. The final of the Half Mile Foot Handicap produced a keen race, and H. Richards, Ammanford, who appeared to be losing ground, and wearing badly on the second lap, suddenly surprised the crowd with a sprint, and gaining premier place maintained it to the end and won by a yard. The Half Mile Cycle Handicap saw a splendid finish between Hughes, Brynaman, and Nicholas, Hopkinstown. The former took the lead on the home straight, but Nicholas, who appeared to be a mere youngster, was not to be denied, and, riding grandly, won by barely half a wheel. In the 300 Yards Flat Foot Handicap, after seven heats, with such a large number of short markers appearing the race was exceptionally keen, and there was a great fight for position on the bend. Morgan, Penrhiwceiber, who reserved himself for the last 50 yards, made a dash and went "all out." He overtook Griffiths, Merthyr, about two yards from the finishing post, palpably shaking on his legs, and collided with Griffiths. The latter went to the ground and there were shouts of "foul", but from the press table which was in line with the two runners, it was evident that Morgan unintentionally upset his co-competitor. In any case he would have won, and the judges took the view that there was no "intention" and awarded him the race. Todd, Australia, was third, and D. Roberts, Edinburgh, fourth. Arthur Postle, the world's champion sprinter, met with an accident just previous to Saturday, spraining his thigh. In course of conversation on Monday he spoke in most appreciative terms of the fine running track at Pontypridd and the reception which had been accorded him on his advent to the coalopolis last week. "It is an ideal Ground", he remarked, "for the people can see from every point. I predict a grand future for the Welsh sprint, for it is managed so methodically and there are such a decent lot of fellows connected with it. Mr. Ted Lewis is a very careful handicapper. This advantage is most necessary, and goes a long way to the success of such meetings. I have some experience" added Postle, modestly "of race meetings, but I have never know such a programme carried out so minutely to scheduled time as they do at Pontypridd. I really believe I could not show my proper form by a long way. I really believe I had a chance to win if it had not been for my injury."

The Wallabies Win At Taff Vale Park

On December 17th 1908, the touring Australian Rugby Union team played the Glamorgan League team at Taff Vale Park. The league had been in existence since 1894 after the suggestion of Pontypridd RFC secretary, Teddy Lewis, who was of course a member of the Athletic Syndicate, and this was probably their most important fixture since that date. The Taff Vale Ground on the day was in a very sodden condition, and to make matters worse a heavy downpour was experienced just before the kick-off, and as a result there were numerous small ponds on the field. Considering the importance of the match the attendance was disappointing, for at the start there were not more than 2,000 spectators present. Woods, the Australian captain, got the ball away from successive early scrums, and Dix put in good work on the left wing. Then the home forwards brought off some nice passing until Granville broke through very nicely, but Davies knocked on. Fine passing by the Australian threequarters ended in W. Dix dodging the opposing backs to score behind the posts, for Carmichael to add the extra points. Soon after, Morgan made a great dribble, and the home backs started a smart movement, and J. Caple, receiving the ball eight yards from the line, and finding only one opponent before him, did the right thing in not passing, and when tackled plunged over for an unconverted try. The league team played a surprisingly good game and were only trailing 5-3 at the interval. There were about 3,000 present at the restart, and Dix soon got over again for Australia, but the pass was forward, but then Mandible scored an unconverted try from an opening by Wood. The home fullback did some magnificent tackling, and once stopped Russell magnificently when all the other defenders had been beaten.

M'Kivett made a clever burst, and when tackled two yards from the line by Griffiths (Penygraig) managed to get the ball away to Row, who scored another unconverted try. At halfway, Row got the ball on the fringes of a scrum and ran through the league backs, but Griffiths, who had played heroically for the home side, had to leave the field through injury. Final Score: Glamorgan League 3 pts Australia 11 pts.

Australia: Back, P. Carmichael; Threequarters, W. Dix, A. J. M'Cabe, E. Mandible, C. Russell; Halves, F .Woods + M'Kivett; Forwards, Barnett, Griffin, M'Arthur, Burge, Murtrie, Gavin, Row + Craig.

Glamorgan League: Back, D. G. Griffiths (Penygraig), Threequarters, D. Davies (Llwynypia), J. Donovan (Mountain Ash), J. Parker (Llwynypia), H. Gravelle (Mountain Ash); Halves, D. Mead (Llwynypia) + Wyndham Jones (Mountain Ash); Forwards, P. C. Dick Thomas (Mountain Ash), W. Morgan (Treorchy), J. Polsom (Treorchy), Gordon Eustace (Treorchy), Morgan Griffiths (Pontypridd) Evan Evans (Penygraig), J. Caple (Mountain Ash), M. Coleman (Maesteg).

1909

The Pontypridd Observer of May 15th 1909 reported that the Pontypridd Athletic Club had decided to hold sports meetings every fortnight throughout the summer at the Taff Vale Park, and that they had done much to improve the grounds, and amongst the latest additions was a grandstand at the town end.

Whitsun 1909 - Newport to Pontypridd Marathon

All the other sports on Whit-Monday 1909 shrank into comparative insignificance before the Newport to Pontypridd Marathon Contest. Councillor David Williams and his fellow organisers had displayed the thoroughness and regard for detail for which the Pontypridd Athletic Club had become proverbial, and no possible arrangement for the success of the race had been neglected. Every entrant to the race had to submit to a medical examination by Dr. Howard Davies, who accordingly followed the competitors in a motor car to watch for any possible signs of fatigue. A car had also been provided for the conveyance back to Pontypridd of any of the competitors who showed signs of exhaustion. The competitors got off promptly at 2 o'clock from the Pill Harriers ground, Newport. Amongst those competing were: Fred Lord, who represented England at Olympia, and who had three times come second in marathon events; John Price, winner of the Cheltenham marathon; D. Jones, Mardy; B. D. Christmas, Llandebie; W. Dixey, Newport; G. Powell and G. Spanwick, Cwmbran; Angelo Butti, Commo, Italy; A. H. Waygood, Pontypridd, W. T. J. Weston & J. H. Evans, Caerphilly; T. E. Harry, Cardiff; A. T. Yeoumans, Worlds Champion walker; C. Gould, Cardiff; J. Croin, Rhydyfelin, M. Murphy & James Parfitt, Pontypridd; James Roberts, Sefton Harriers, the world's record holder over the full distance of 26¼ miles. The start was witnessed by a large crowd and the positions by Castletown were Spanwick, Gould, Lord, Martin; at Cardiff, Gould, Christmas, Lord. Even at this early stage a number of the competitors showed signs of fatigue and some had already abandoned the contest. At Cardiff, Lord spurted ahead and walked strongly along the next stage to Whitchurch. Price now made the running and was only 5 yards behind Lord at Taffs Well, and passed him on reaching Upper Boat. The Cheltenham winner continued to hold the premier position from this stage , increasing his lead until Taff Vale Park was reached. Tremendous applause greeted the arrival of the leader at the park and Price had completed 1½ laps when Lord appeared, followed threequarters of a lap later by Roberts. Christmas, the Llandebie man, was loudly cheered on his arrival. The following men were the winners:

1. - J. Price 2 hrs. 22 mins; 2. - F. Lord 2 hrs. 24 mins; 3. - J. Roberts, 2 hrs. 25 mins; 4. - B. D. Christmas 2 hrs. 29 mins; 5. - T. E. Harry, 2 hrs. 42 mins; 6. - D. Spanwick, 2 hrs. 44 mins; 7. - A. T. Yeoumans - No official time. These were the only competitors out of the 18 who completed the course, the majority having retired between Cardiff and Taffs Well. Some other excellent contests were witnessed, including: - One Mile Novice Handicap, 120 Yards Flat Handicap, Half Mile Cycle Handicap; 120 Yards Hurdles; 440 Yards

The Greyhound Inn, H.Q. of the Welsh Powderhall, Circa 1905

Flat Handicap; and a High Jump Handicap, won by W. R. Hughes, Porth, from 3 in, who cleared 5ft 1 inch. On Whit-Tuesday 1909, another professional sports under the auspices of the Athletic Club took place. An innovation in the programme was the introduction of a Trotting Handicap. The number of entrants marked an easy record, thus proving the popularity of this meeting, there being over 100 in one event alone., and it spoke well for the thoroughness of the arrangements that at six o'clock fully a quarter of an hour had been gained on the scheduled time. A feature of the meeting was the evident encouragement given by the officials to long distance racing, especially in the cycling department, and the result amply justified the experiment, the finishes not only in the finals, but even in the heats proving very exciting. E. C. Newman, of Treforest, was the successful competitor in the Two Mile Cycle Handicap, and his performance pointed to his soon becoming one of the leading crack riders. Amongst the others who carried off honours were the old favourites, Churchill, Penygraig and Hill, Cardiff. The one event, however, which eclipsed all others was the Half Mile Flat Handicap, when Davies, of Tenby, who was well known on the Taff Vale Park, consequent upon his previous brilliant performances on the ground, all but succeeded in passing two-dozen men who were in front of him, and excitement ran high as it was seen by the outburst of encouraging cheers when he was getting up to the first man. In the One Mile Flat Handicap, run in one heat, H. Wooledge, London, the crack cross country runner, being back marker, was going along splendidly when, to the chagrin of the spectators, he met with an accident, and had to give up, and A. R. Hodgkinson, Ogmore vale, won off 110 yards. On the whole the meeting was regarded as one of the best of the many successful meetings that had been held by the Athletic club.

August Bank Holiday 1909

As usual with this bank Holiday programme the amateur sports were held on Monday and the professional sports on Tuesday. A feature of the former was the appearance on the track of R. E. Walker, South Africa, the youthful world's sprinting champion, who intended attacking the world 100 Yard Flat Handicap record. It was also his ambition to break the record for 120 yards. He was given a cordial reception on his proceeding to the track, which was in excellent condition. He had expressed his entire satisfaction with the track, the condition of which was as such as to materially assist in a record being created on the Pontypridd ground. Unfortunately he failed to gain his object in either respect. In the 100 Yards race Walker made a magnificent effort, and in the heat was first to reach the tape, covering the distance in 10 secs; and the excitement was intense when the final was run, as the chances were quite even up to the very time that the tape was broken. Indeed, so close were the first four runners that it was impossible for the spectators to see who was the actual winner, but was finally announced as E. Davies, Grange, off 10 yards. In the 120 Yards Race Walker did not start well in his heat and though he made headway, Gunstone, of Llanishen, just managed to beat him. However, E. Davies, off 13½ Yards, brought off a magnificent double by winning this event, with Ponter, Newport, second and Waite, St Saviour's, third.

The Ten Mile Flat Scratch Race also attracted a great deal of attention, amongst the class entrants being such well-known runners such as A. J. Robertson, W. H. Day and A. Ashby, of the Birchfield Harriers. The first named being the English national champion in 1908 and came second in the English A.A.A. Four Mile championship at Stamford Bridge, while Day had been an English international runner for the last 5 years. Robertson won the event. Many of the cycling events proved most interesting and exciting. A One Mile Novice Cycle Handicap was won by W. Bowdler, Newport (Scratch); the Half-mile championship of Wales was won by J. Hill, Cardiff, while the Half Mile Cycle Handicap saw F. Williams, Abercwmboi, emerge winner. The Five Mile Cycle Championship of Wales was won by J. Jeremiah, Newport.

The programme for the professional sports on Tuesday was, if anything, more attractive. There was a large field of competitors, and there could scarcely have been better finishes in the foot or cycle events. There was only one heat wherein the competitors displayed indifference - the One Mile Cycle Handicap - and the referee, councillor David Williams, at once ordered the whole of the riders to dismount, and they were disqualified. This prompt decision was an earnest ambition of the Pontypridd Athletic Club to insist upon the straight running in every event. The cycling competitions proved some magnificent racing and clever judgement in manoeuvring for positions, and in this category the riding in the Five-Mile Championship stood out as the feature of the day, and Newman, Pontypridd, who won from such experienced strategists as Churchill and Hughes, was deservedly applauded for his sound generalship. Fourteen riders turned out for this event, and a hot pace was set from the start, the competitors being in a group until the last lap. Newman, who had kept a good position in the leading three men, forged ahead 300 yards from the tape, being challenged by Hughes, Brynaman, and T. Churchill. A desperate struggle ensued on the home straight, but Newman rode superbly and won by two lengths, defeating Churchill who was much fancied, somewhat easily, Hughes coming third. Those two popular cracks, F. C. Davies, Tenby, and B. R. Day, Blackpool (the 1908 Welsh Powderhall winner), gave splendid performances in their heats, though they failed to gain any of the bigger prizes. Day in the finish of the 300 Yards avoided what must have proved an ugly accident by making a clear jump over a collapsed comrade when going at full tilt. The final was won by F. White Penygraig, off 40 yards. Day made a great effort, but was locked in, and had to check his stride. He, however, got through cleverly and gained third prize amid applause. The 120 Yards Flat Handicap drew a field of nearly 100 competitors, and young J. S. Isaacs, Mountain Ash, who finished first, showed plenty of grit and went all out. The Trotting Handicap, which proved one of the features of the programme, brought out 12 of the best horses in South Wales, and some pretty running was witnessed, the winner being "Lady" off 450 yards, owned by W. Evans, Pontypridd. The 120 Yards Novice Flat Handicap was won by L. Davies Pontypridd, off 12 yards. The 880 Yards Flat Handicap was won by J. J. Evans, Pontypridd, off 85 yards.

Boxing And An Exhibition Of Endurance

The Pontypridd Observer of August 14th 1909, gave the following account of a boxing contest at Taff Vale Park on the previous Monday, August 9th: -

'On Monday night, in company with many others, I paid a visit to the Taff Vale Park - the pet child of Councillor David Williams. The worthy councillor is never happier than when he is beautifying and improving the park, and there is no doubt that in a few years it will be a very pretty spot, where jaded citizens may stroll of an evening under the shade of the trees, listening to the band, and the younger members of the community can worship the goddess Terpisichore and trip the light fantastic to their hearts content. It was not with this object we wended our way on Monday. It was to see an exhibition of endurance and skill. It is true we observed the endurance, two men pummelling each other for one hour - but we were not sufficiently versed in the noble art to observe the skill. On getting inside I observed a crowd, many holding responsible positions in the town. But on entering the grandstand I was not so favourably impressed. Many were bookmakers and ex-fighters.

Opposite the grandstand was the ring - a square ring - a stage erected on barrels enclosed by ropes. On the boards was a magnificent piece of linoleum, on which a man could fall without bruising himself. If it cost a penny it cost nearly £5. Around were a few sheets to prevent the people of the Common having a free view. About 7 o'clock the two men, accompanied by their seconds, entered the ring, also the referee, a gentleman whose hair was grey, but who had a lot of walking to about and parting to do in the course of the contest. The two men were Eddie Carsey, an American, and Jimmy Southway, Pentre. The crowd seemed to favour Jimmy, but Carsey was the man that the "experts" believed would pull off the event. Freddy Welsh was there as one of Carsey's sponsors. Well, to come to the point, the men set to. In the first ten rounds they appeared to be chiefly engaged in embracing each other. These loving overtures did not meet with the approval of the referee, who was continually engaged either in warning the men or parting them. "Cuddling each other" he called it. When they reached the fourteenth round there was a sign of business and both men showed a greater desire to fight. Southway got his eye nearly closed and both men got severely punished. Southway's blows seemed to lack weight but Casey's were nine pounders. At the 20th round the referee declared the fight a draw as "he could not part these men." What is to be learnt from a contest of this kind? First of all it shows what men can endure, but is such endurance of any real good? It is well for every Britisher to be able to use his fists should the occasion require it - for instance if his castle is invaded by mid-night marauders, or if he is waylaid on a lonely road, but in a fairly civilised country like this the ordinary man has no occasion to become a trained boxer. Physical culture, in moderation is good, and should be encouraged, but it is very doubtful if the present wave of enthusiasm in favour of boxing does not raise the brute in the spectators. The syndicate are determined that any encounters that take place on their grounds shall be properly conducted and if there is any ruffianism or foul play, a contest will be stopped at once. '

On Monday evening, August 23rd 1909, a Half Mile race, billed as the World championship, was held at Taff Vale Park between B. R. Day of Blackpool, and F. C. Davies, of Tenby, and aroused tremendous interest, as both runners were well-known and very popular in Welsh athletic circles. During the last five years both competitors had frequently appeared in the Taff Vale Park, Day having competed on numerous occasions in the sprints, and the previous year had won the Welsh Powderhall Handicap after a remarkable finish. Day had always been considered more of a sprinter than a long distance runner, and his most conspicuous performances had been made in the 120, 130, and 300 Yard Handicaps. Though Day had figured at long distances he had not met with great success. On the other hand Davies was essentially a half-miler. He possessed excellent stamina, and was invariably a remarkably strong finisher. He had made some exceptionally good times over grass tracks, and the conditions prevailing on Monday night were considered to favour the Tenbyite. Davies had beaten all the crack runners, and he was particularly favoured for the race. The track had been specially prepared by the Pontypridd Syndicate, the grass having been cut quite short like a cricket pitch and rolled well, but despite this the rain during recent days had made it rather heavy going, and it was expected that a record time would not be accomplished. Both men were on the mark almost promptly to time, and as both men made the preliminaries down the course they met with cheers from their respective partisans, the Welshmen apparently being the favourite with the crowd. The men were got well off their marks by the starter, Mr. Ted Lewis. In the first ten yards Davies forged ahead amid the cheers of the crowd. He widened the distance to two yards, and both men were running easily in this position for the first quarter mile. Day somewhat reduced the lead of his rival at the end of the first lap, but Davies again went well ahead. About 240 yards from home when approaching the last bend on the track, Day made a spurt and got ahead of the Welshman. Davies, however, was not to be denied, and with a big effort he got his inside position and amid tremendous excitement he gained ground inch by inch until he was nearly four yards ahead of Day. Accident alone could now prevent Davies from winning, as he was quite fresh, while Day was palpably tiring, and in the next 50 yards Davies was going so strongly that Day discovered that it was a hopeless task, and a hundred yards from home he retired. Davies never looked back, but went at full tilt, and was cheered vociferously for his magnificent victory. During the evening there was a 120 Yard Novice Flat Handicap of three rounds, including the final, won by Dan Davies, Treherbert.

Welsh Powderhall 1909

Owing to a continual downpour on Saturday the heats of the great 130 Yards Open Handicap, the Welsh Powderhall, were postponed until Monday. It must have consoled the Pontypridd Athletic Syndicate to see the large crowd who presented themselves on Monday and Tuesday. All the cracks from both hemispheres were entrants and the only absentee was Postle of Australia, who was suffering from a strained ankle. The starters included Growcott, of Banbury; Day, of Blackpool, last years winner; Eastman, the Canadian; Holway, of America, as well as the foremost runners of the principality. Much to the surprise of a large section of the crowd,

S. Williams, of Tenby, a much fancied man to win outright, was defeated in his heat by T. G. Thomas, Pencoed. The local men did not figure prominently, not a single Pontypriddian succeeding in winning a heat. With all the crack runners left in there was every prospect of excellent racing on the second day. B. Saunders, of Pontyclun, was first favourite. Those acquainted with the marvellous running powers of Holway, the U.S.A flyer, however, felt fairly confident that he would "do the trick". Heat 1 in the second round was won by R. O. Rees, 10 Yards, who defeated both Day and Growcott (both 1½ yards). The second was won by T. G. Thomas, Pencoed, but the third was a capital race, the back marker, A. Peebles, Edinburgh, 6½ Yds, being just defeated by F. J. Thomas, Pontymoel, who finished at great pace. The fourth and final heat was the most hotly contested, containing as it did both first and second favourites C. E. Holway, 2½ Yards, and B. Saunders, 15½ Yards, both men being heavily backed. The heat proved a surprise to many in Holway overtaking Saunders twenty yards from the tape, his serious rival being Frowd, of Newport, 7 Yards, who was hardly a yard behind Holway when the latter breasted the tape. Great excitement prevailed when the final was being run, and of the four finalists Holway, was the favourite, odds of 6 to 4 being freely laid. Rees of Glanaman, for some time seemed to be making a good bid for the laurels, but Thomas, of Pontymoel, dashed ahead and Holway snatched a hard fought victory from him. On Monday the One Mile Scratch Cycle Race for the Professional Championship of the South Wales Centre, was won by E. C. Newman, Treforest.

600 Yards Championship of the World

Taff Vale Park on Monday September 27th 1909 was not so well attended to witness the 600 Yards Championship Race of the World between F. C. Davies, Tenby, and B. R. Day, Blackpool, as on the previous occasion when the pair ran on the same grounds for the Half Mile Championship of the World. The race started well, Davies leading until about half the course had been traversed. Day then passed him keeping about 2 or 3 yards ahead of him until he breasted the tape which was done amidst the cheers of the crowd.

There was also a 120 Yards Open Handicap, the winner being W. Fearnley, Cardiff.

Two cycle races which created a great deal of interest were decided at the Taff Vale Park on Monday evening, October 1st 1909, between Charles Newman, Treforest, and Tom Churchill, of Penygraig. The latter had previously won a number of championships under the auspices of the South Wales Centre, but on the last occasion of a championship race at Taff Vale Park Newman defeated him. The outcome was a challenge to Newman, which was accepted, and on this date they contested a Half Mile and Quarter Mile Cycle Pursuit race for £50 aside - £25 on each race. The first race was over the half mile distance, Churchill being favourite. Mr. David Williams was the referee and starter. Newman with the crack of the pistol got off the mark splendidly, and after the first 50 yards it was seen that he was gaining on his opponent and was fully six yards to the good before a quarter of the distance had been done. This lead he not only maintained, but increased in the next 400 yards, and won with 15 yards to spare. In the second race, Newman was the favourite, and he justified the confidence of his supporters by again achieving victory. Churchill in this race had the misfortune to steer on to the grass track, which put him out of his stride, and claimed a re-run. The articles signed by the runners made no reference to an accident of this nature, and the referee had no option but to declare Newman the winner. The victor was then carried shoulder high by his supporters amid loud cheering.

1910

Easter 1910 - Galloway a Success

The annual Easter sports programme took place on Easter Monday and Tuesday, and included a Tug-of war event. On Tuesday there were the usual Professional Foot, Cycling and Whippet Handicaps, but undoubtedly the greatest attraction was the new horse track. This track, on which trotting and galloway races would be held, had been constructed that winter outside the cycle track at the cost of several hundred pounds, and the promoters of the sports at Taff Vale Park claimed that it was the finest track in Wales, being nearly a third of a mile in circumference. Although the weather on Monday morning, April 25th 1910 was anything but pleasurable for outdoor sports, in the afternoon it cleared up, and became quite enjoyable, causing a good many persons to attend the sports at the Taff Vale grounds. It was gratifying to note that the new horse track, which had been recently constructed at a big expense, was proving an attraction. No less than twenty horses entered for the Galloway races and some exciting finishes were witnessed.

Whitsun 1910

Tremendous entries had been received for the Pontypridd Athletic Club's sports on Whit-Tuesday and Wednesday, May 16th and 17th 1910. The professional foot and cycle events received good attention from the athletes as it was only to be expected when one considered the value of the prizes offered. For the £130 Sprint nearly ninety entries had been received. The heats of this race were run on Tuesday and the semi-finals and final on Wednesday. Excellent entries were also received for all the other foot events, and in the cycle events great interest was shown owing to the first appearance of Syd Jenkins, who had not ridden for some time. J. S. Benyon, the professional cycle champion, E. C. Newman, G. Sheen, etc, also competed. Over forty entries had been received for the Whippet Handicap. On Wednesday a fine programme of horse events was arranged, together with some cycling, and the finals of the 120 Yards Handicap, and the 130 Yards Handicap. All the trotting and galloway events were well supported with entries from all part of South Wales and the West of England, and the majority of the favourite Welsh horses put in an appearance. Great interest was also shown in the new departure of the Pontypridd Athletic Club, viz; the offering of prizes for the best dressed business horses. It was hoped that the promoters would make this an annual competition, so that the drivers of horses in and around Pontypridd would be sufficiently stimulated to look after their horses well during the year, so that they may capture the valuable silver cups which were offered.

Pontypridd Athletic Club - Grand Two Day Meeting

Amongst those who sent in entries for these events and competed over the two days of Saturday July 2nd and Monday July 4th 1910, was the famous "Major" Taylor, of Tasmania, who was credited with having done the 100 Yards in 9.25 seconds, a truly wonderful performance, equalling the time returned the previous year for the same distance by Donaldson in South Africa; for which performance the colonial was the holder of the world record over that distance. For some time past Taylor's health had been indifferent, and this, coupled with the effect of Saturday's cold air, probably accounted for the fact that the crack failed to distinguish himself in his heat of the 120 Yards Sprint. Taylor, who was scratch man, failed to overtake the allowance men, and the heat was won comfortably by J. Mathias, Ferndale, who started off the 19 yards mark. There were 61 entries, who competed in ten heats. The colonial did better in his heat for the 300 Yards, but even here he failed to finish first or second, in one of four heats, and thus did not qualify for the final. There were 13 entries for the Half Mile Professional Cycle Handicap, which was run in three heats. The final on Saturday was won by E. Burgess, Porth. In the One Mile Galloway Open Handicap, four heats of six were run. The young jockey on "little maid", from Merthyr, was thrown, but escaped any serious damage.

On Monday, Major Taylor, though easily winning his heat, and though making a brilliant effort, was unsuccessful in the final of the 220 Yards Foot Handicap. He forged ahead steadily, but was unable to overtake the winners before reaching the tape, though he was very close to their heels. In the 300 Yards Foot Handicap F. C. Davies, of Tenby, was a popular winner. The 120 Yards Foot Handicap was won by T. H. Oldfield, of Cardiff, amid the plaudits of the crowd. The Amateur Half Mile Foot Handicap proved a magnificent race. J. Hill - though winning his heat easily, had little to spare in the final, so keenly was the event contested. The galloway races also aroused a great deal of interest. This innovation by the Athletic club had proved so successful that these races would probably be run at most future events.

The Glamorgan Free Press of July 22nd 1910 disclosed that Jack Donaldson, Australia and C. E. Holway, America, had agreed to run 130 Yards for £100 aside and a purse of £200 offered by the Pontypridd Athletic Club at the Taff Vale Park on August bank holiday. The side stakes and the purse were deposited with the "Sports Chronicle ", who would appoint all officials for the match. The club, too, on the day of the race, intended holding a sports prior to the match, consisting of professional foot events, and amateur cycle events, and all the great athletes in the country were expected to come to Pontypridd in order to witness the match, and a great entry was anticipated for these sports, and for the galloway event which would be held on Tuesday. That same day Donaldson would again be in evidence, as he endeavoured to lower the world record for a circular grass track. It is of interest to know that all the entries for both days sports included, besides Donaldson, Holway, Major Taylor, Tasmania; Eastman, Canada; B. R. Day, Blackpool; F. C. Davies, Tenby; Peebles, Cowan and Henderson, Edinburgh; Muir, Rochdale. Cycle events - J. S. Benyon, P. R. Quinlan, South Africa; Syd Jenkins, E. C. Newman, Welsh Champion; T. Churchill, T. Williams and King, Birmingham; and C. E. Baker, Carmarthen.

World's Sprint Championship

The World's Sprint Championship over a distance of 130 Yards was decided after a memorable race on Monday, August 1st 1910, at the Taff Vale Park, under the auspices of the Pontypridd Athletic Club when C. E. Holway, of America, raced Jack Donaldson of Australia. Prior to the great race an excellent programme was gone through, and several of the events, both cycling, and foot, proved exceptionally interesting, some of the finishes being most exciting. The 120 Yards flat handicap was notable for the appearance of Eastman, the famous Canadian, and Major Taylor, the equally famous Tasmanian runner. The former was the scratch man, and just lost his heat after a magnificent effort. Taylor came in for thunderous applause in winning his heat. In the second round, however, though making a splendid effort, he was knocked out. The cycling events proved equally interesting. The One Mile Scratch was secured by T. Williams, Abercwmboi, who also secured a second in the Half Mile Cycle Handicap. W. H. Kerr, of Birmingham, secured premier honours in both Quarter and Half Mile Handicaps. The big race, however, had aroused the keenest interest in athletic circles, and provided a great attraction, a large crowd, estimated around 7,000, gathered to witness the contest. the spectators expected a rare treat in witnessing the race. It was evident that the greatest excitement prevailed. Upon the appearance of Donaldson on the field they gave vent to their pent-up feelings, by giving him a mighty cheer, a similar compliment being accorded Holway upon his emerging from the dressing room ready for the contest. Although quite impartial in their plaudits, Holway seemed the favourite from the start. Indeed, Holway, since his capture of a premier prize of £140 at the Welsh Powderhall on the Taff Vale Grounds last September, had always been a great favourite at Pontypridd meetings. His chances, however, were not regarded as altogether rosy.

As the time for the big event drew near the greatest excitement prevailed, and in the meantime the officials were making the necessary preparations, Mr. Redding, of the "Sporting Chronicle," being the special referee, Mr. Hepplewaite, the pistol firer. Both runners made trial expeditions over the cinder track. It was noticed that Donaldson had a wide bandage on his right thigh, while Holway had the same. Punctually at six o'clock the men were in position, and a dead silence prevailed and instantly the pistol was fired. Both men simply flew off the mark, but Donaldson was palpably the smarter in this initial stage, and kept his slight lead for about 20 yards. The American in the ensuing 30 or 40 yards made slight, but appreciable headway, and as the two men ran abreast for all that they were worth, it seemed as if the issue would be undecided, and the uncertainties of the situation only added to the tense excitement of the crowd. When the men were about 40 or 50 yards from the tape, and still absolutely abreast of each other, Donaldson's stride seemed to falter, and Holway gained an advantage, but it was simply momentary, and the Australian did not relax an iota in a desperate effort to win the event. When at last the tape was broken, so close together were the two men that the crowd was quite unable to adjudge the victor, and this proved an additional exciting element. It was not, indeed, until the referee ran up to Holway and patted him that it was known that he was the victor, and instantly he was hailed with a tremendous cheer. With commendable sportsmanlike spirit Donaldson was the first to give a congratulatory handshake to his rival - an action which elicited another outburst of applause on the part of the spectator , and both Holway and Donaldson came in for a great ovation on their retirement to the dressing-room. It had been anticipated that a better time would have been recorded, but it must be remembered the runners had to contend against a strong head wind, and, under the circumstances, their achievement was a good one. It was recognised on all hands that the race was magnificent, and that both men had given an exhibition worthy of their reputations in the athletic world.

On Tuesday, the very unfavourable weather militated greatly against a good attendance. The events were: - 120 Yards Flat Handicap, won by L. Williams, Tonypandy, off 16 Yards; Quarter Mile Cycle Handicap, won by G. Sheen, Cardiff; Half Mile Cycle Handicap, won by Edmunds, Penygraig off 66 Yards; 440 Yards Open Flat Handicap, won by Carey, Cardiff off 41 Yards, Five Mile Cycle Championship of S.W. Centre, won by G. Sheen, and One Mile Open Galloway, won by "Llangan May," Llangan. But the big event that day was the 120 Yards Open Flat Handicap, which after seven heats was won in the final by S. J. Thomas, Aberaman, off 16½ yards, with Mills, Porth, second off 11½ yards, and Eastman was third.

Welsh Powderhall 1910

On Saturday, Aug 27th 1910, long before the time announced for the first event the grounds were well filled, testifying in no uncertain manner to the enthusiastic interest aroused in sporting circles. The men of the valleys are noted for their love of sport, and although the weather appeared threatening, there were upwards of 5,000 assembled and the grand stand was crowded. There was not only the big Welsh Sprint, the Welsh Powderhall, but also two other good events. The One Mile Scratch Cycle Championship, brought an entry of 15. All four heats proved good contests, and in the final

C.E. Newman, of Treforest, the holder of the championship, after a stiff struggle was defeated by Syd Jenkins of Abercynon. In the Half Mile Foot Handicap, for the first prize of £20 and a gold medal, this event drew forth an entry of 76. After the heats of over 14 men, the first three in each heat went through to the final on Monday.

The 130 Yards Foot Handicap, in which in addition to the substantial prizes for the first four men, a prize of £1 was given to the winner of each of the twenty heats, and drew an entry of 97 men of note and fairly eclipsed all the rest of the programme. The finishes, many of them, were most exciting and caused great enthusiasm, and the onerous task of the handicapping proved to have been most carefully and fairly carried out. A good point, too, was the fact that in order to win their heats the scratch men and the short markers had to cover the track within evens, this providing good sport for the big crowd that assembled.

On Monday, a very big crowd, even more in number than on Saturday, assembled to witness the semi-finals and final of the Welsh Sprint. It was estimated that about 8,000 persons were present. The first event was the Half Mile Cycle Handicap, and after four heats of 18 entries, was won by A. Harris, Pembroke Dock. The final of the 800 Yards Foot Handicap was won easily by J. J. Evans. The 300 Yards Foot Handicap saw 114 entries divided into four heats, and the final was won by Henderson, 16 Yds, of Edinburgh. Also in the heats were J. Donaldson, Australia; B. R. Day, Blackpool; Nat Cartmell, America; E. Eastman, Canada; Major Taylor, Tasmania; and A. P. Postle, Australia. However, all the famous names went out in the heats and four semi-finals, and the final was contested by Hanford, Blaengwynfi; T. G. Thomas, Pencoed; J. Lloyd, Dowlais; Henderson, Edinburgh; A. Peebles, Portobello; M. T. Evans, Treforest, P. S. Thomas, Cardiff and F. J. Carey, Cardiff. In the final the first prize of £20 and a gold medal given by Mr. E. Powell of the White Hart Hotel, was easily won by Henderson by a couple of yards, and Carey was less than a couple of yards in front of Hanford, who was third man, with J. Lloyd fourth.

Very seldom had there been so much enthusiasm in sporting circles as that witnessed over the final of the big sprint. Major Taylor was the strong favourite on Monday, notwithstanding his performance on Saturday, therefore it was a great surprise to see him beaten in the heats by Oldfield. The coloured champion's supporters were disappointed in his failure to appear in the final through losing his semi-final. There seemed to be a stroke of hard ill-luck for the "big cracks", for Donaldson, the Australian, a winner on Saturday, had a sprained thigh, and this prevented him trying conclusions on Monday. At the conclusion of the semi-finals, Thomas, of Merthyr. became the great favourite. Holway had acted as his coach, and this fact greatly helped his popularity. Oldfield's victory over Major Taylor in the fourth semi-final heat was somewhat of a surprise, but, all the same, he ran a glorious race. It was neck and neck between the Cardiffian and Powell, Tredegar, all the way, and at the tape Oldfield gained the verdict by a foot. Major Taylor was nearly three yards off for third place. In the final, Winsper, Darleston, 10½ Yds; W. Thomas, Merthyr, 14 Yds; T. W. Meredith, Cardiff, 12 Yds; and Oldfield, Cardiff, 3 Yds - got well away at the start, and great excitement ensued when it was seen that Thomas, who was the long marker, was actually holding his own, and at the half-way all competitors were relatively in their starting positions, Thomas leading by a yard and Meredith and Oldfield making a grim struggle to overtake him. Winsper was fully 2½ yards behind, and his chances were soon regarded as hopeless, for the other three men were running very strongly. When he was thirty yards from the tape Thomas was all over a winner. The general excitement of the whole assembly culminated in loud bursts of applause and cheer after cheer as Thomas continued to keep his premier position and finish as victor, winning by a yard with Meredith as second, and a foot in front of Oldfield, behind whom, about a yard away, was Winsper. The winners of all the heats had been most heartily cheered and enthusiastically received by their supporters, and Thomas's achievement appeared to be a most popular one. Looking back over the two days sports it was said that they had been amongst the best that the enterprising Pontypridd Athletic Club had provided for the public of South Wales.

Pontypridd Cottage Hospital - Successful Carnival

In order to endeavour to open the new cottage hospital at Pontypridd free of debt, a very special effort was being made to increase the subscriptions. One of the methods employed was that of a Grand Carnival, with competitions and prizes. This was held on Saturday afternoon, September 24th 1910. The rendezvous was the Taff Vale Park, and it was satisfactory to report that there was a good attendance of the public. The new horse-trotting track made a very good place for the assemblage of the procession before it emerged from the grounds to proceed around the town. The scene in the grounds was a very pretty and gay one. There were numbers of gaily dressed children, young women, and young men, garbed in the costumes of many nations; also comic characters, and the usual collection seen at masquerades. Besides these there were over twenty equestrians, knights in armour, gay cavaliers, cowboys and girls, clowns etc. Then there were the ambulance brigades from the Great Western, Albion, and Maritime, Penrhiw and Lady Windsor Collieries; the girls of the St. Matthews Red Cross Brigade; and the St Matthews Church Lads Brigade, and two troops of the Pontypridd Boy Scouts. Specially worthy of note amongst the "maskers" were a group which a gigantic white Leghorne cockerel was drawing on an ornamental floral carriage, in which was a chicken emerging from a shell; the whole was in charge of four fairies dressed in white, as a further bodyguard they had three moorish princesses. The flying circle had its votaries, for there was a somewhat large aeroplane, about twelve foot long, with propeller in action. This was built very skilfully so as to include a bicycle, on which it moved from place to place A notice on the machine intimated that the builders were prepared to build aeroplanes from £10,000 each, but they would not guarantee that they would fly! There was also a miniature biplane, with a child's tricycle incorporated into it. Possibly the visit of three Russians to the town with two performing bears earlier in the week inspired one competitor to dress in the garb of a Russian and shoulder a large "Teddy Bear," such as were now seen in grocers shops as the advertisement of a certain firm of biscuit makers. One of the most striking characters was that of "Dr. Price," who appeared in his well-remembered fur cap, beard, sash, trousers, and flaming torch. Before the procession started there were some competitions, in which about thirty mothers competed with their "treasures"; there was one proud father who stood with his child amongst the mothers, and seemed especially desirous that his offspring should carry off one of the prizes. On the authority of a lady guardian, who acted as one of the judges, we can say they were "a beautiful lot of babies." This was followed by various competitions amongst which the Church Lad's Brigade, and then the three squads of the Red Cross Brigade Girls went through their ambulance drill. After these events there was a surprise in store. Two midget boxers, aged about three years, in orthodox costumes, were brought into the field and commenced, after some coaxing, to "Bang" one another. Their names were Johnnie Godwin and Sydney Pugh, of Taylor's Terrace, Tram Road. There were also several decorated dogs, who bore collection boxes as panniers.

As the procession emerged from the grounds the officials entered a carriage, and preceded by two mounted constables and the town band, headed the cavalcade, which between Taff Vale Park and the station square was joined by a large number of tradesmen's decorated carts, wagons, and a pit pony drawing a tram of coal. This latter proved a rather difficult vehicle to guide along roads without tramlines. As the procession turned from Mill St into Gelliwasted road they were joined by another procession from Trehafod. Altogether there were about 140 persons in fancy dress. The Great Western Colliery sent a working blacksmith's shop, on a lorry, for which Mr. Phillip Williams received an extra prize when they returned to Taff Vale Park. Not only were the men at work forging shoes, but there was a customer waiting for them - a pit pony, who had done 18 years in the pit. He was occasionally rather troublesome. The lorry was drawn by two strong horses, who greatly resented being pulled up every now and again by the procession having to "mark time." After the prize giving on the return to the grounds, the day's festivities aptly concluded with a very good display of fireworks. The display included a very brilliant exhibition of set pieces together with rockets and the latest novelties in the pyrotechnic art. The display was watched by a crowd numbering some 1,000.

The Welsh Powderhall Sprint, Circa 1910

Sprint Championship - Victory For Canadian

The Pontypridd Athletic Club who were always on the alert to provide attractions to Taff Vale Park provided a very good programme on Monday afternoon, September 26th 1910. The chief item was the race between Major Taylor, of Tasmania, and Elderbridge Eastman, the coloured Canadian. The match was described as "for the championship" but for what championship was not clear. The distance was 130 yards. Both men were given a hearty welcome by the spectators, who numbered about 1,000, and a good deal of excitement prevailed during the preliminary arrangements, Taylor being the favourite. Eastman was the smarter in getting off his mark, and secured a short lead, which he retained until half-way. Taylor was here evidently making a desperate and magnificent effort to overtake his rival. He all but succeeded. At one time both men were abreast, but did not continue long is this position. Eastman exerted himself superbly, and was gaining ground appreciably until he had a lead of a yard or two. Major Taylor did not for a moment delay his efforts, and when the contestants reached the tape there was not more than a foot between them. In addition to the championship, £100 was at stake, the stakeholders being the "Evening Express." There were numerous other events, including One and Ten Mile Cycling Championships of the S.Wales Centre, plus the 120 Yards Novice Flat Handicap, and 300 Yards Flat Handicap.

On Saturday Sept 30th 1910 the first Annual Sports in connection with the Berw Road boy scouts was held at the Taff Vale Park. Not only was there a good entry of Pontypridd scouts, but there were also scouts from Taffs Well.

The end of the decade saw athletics, and in particular the Welsh Powderhall, at Taff Vale Park at its peak, with the big event being famous throughout the athletic world, and crowds of several thousand were regular occurrences. They were also catering for local 'pedestrians' with schoolboy races which were included in most of the athletic events and were very popular. Would the Pontypridd Athletic Club, led by the Athletic Syndicate be able to continue this success?

Chapter Four 1911-1914

Soccer Takes Over At T. V. Park

In April 1911, it was announced that it had been decided to form a Professional Association Football Club at Pontypridd. The promoters were already in negotiations with well know players in various parts of the country with a view to signing them for the start of the following season. The establishment of a professional soccer team in the town would mean a football revolution on a small scale if the venture proved successful, and there was every indication that it would. Hitherto rugby had held sway in Pontypridd, and the rugby team that did duty for the old town during the previous season had covered itself in glory by winning the Glamorgan League, but how would the devotees of the "Handling" code fare with "soccerites" disporting themselves in a neighbouring field? The Taff Vale Park, where there was accommodation for around 25,000 and which was one of the finest enclosures in Wales, would be the home ground for the new soccer team.

Easter 1911 - Serious Accident To A Horse

Although the Pontypridd Athletic Club maintained their reputation for supplying a good programme on Easter Tuesday, April 17th 1911, owing to the dull and showery weather there was a very poor attendance. The programme included a 120 Yards Boys Handicap; 120 Yards Flat Open Handicap, which was run in 21 heats and was won by Stoddart, Penygraig; Quarter Mile Cycle Handicap; Half Mile Open Flat Handicap, won by F. J. Carey, Cardiff; One Mile Trotting Handicap, and One Mile Galloway Handicap. A disastrous accident occurred during the preliminary heats of the Galloway Handicap. Whilst going at full speed "Old Dick" the property of Mr. S. Llewellyn, of Aber, who was a favourite, suddenly broke the fetlock of his left front leg, causing his hoof to simply hang by a piece of skin. The jockey was thrown as the horse stumbled, but fortunately was unhurt. The horse had to be destroyed. The final was won by "Mick" owned by Dick Llewellyn, Pontypridd.

1911 Whitsun Sports

The attendance at the 1911 Whit-Monday Sports at the Taff Vale Park was not as large as was usual owing to counter attractions, despite ideal weather and enhanced prizes in foot and horse events. Those who had gathered at the ground had, nevertheless, the pleasure of witnessing some excellent sport. The heat of the 130 Yards Open Flat Handicap attracted Eastman, the celebrated coloured sprinter from Canada, who figured in the list as a late entry, and was scratch man. There were also competing for the prize of £25, B. R. Day, Blackpool; Growcott, Hereford; and Willie Thomas of Merthyr, the last named being the winner of the previous years Powderhall, while Day had gained the coveted prize in 1908. The back-markers, however, were destined to misfortune. Eastman got away badly off his mark, but made a fine effort to overtake Dan Thomas, who had 19 yards start, and got away well on the pistol. T. Meredith, who had 6½ yards the better of B. R. Day, found no difficulty in outdistancing the Blackpool flyer, while Growcott failed to get the measure of E. J. Davies, who had an advantage of 13½ yards on the handicap. The relative performances and marks of the heat winners gave every promise of a close finish in the final. Both Eastman and Day competed in the heats of the 300 Yards Flat Handicap, but again were defeated on the post.

The Half Mile Amateur Cycle Championship of South Wales was productive of a splendid finish, Tom Williams, of Abercwmboi, failing by a length to hold J. Hill, the Cardiffian winning the laurels after a magnificent race. Equally keenly contested was the Half Mile Cycle Handicap, where Bell, Birmingham, won a fine victory over J. Hill, Cardiff. The Two Mile Handicap, which was an exceptionally fine contest, appeared to be anybody's place until the last turn before home, when Bell forged in front of his fellow citizens Lees and Williams, of Abercwmboi, winning from the former by half a length. In the Trotting Handicap for a £25 prize, the victory of the little brindle "Curiosity" was a big surprise to the bookmakers, but not so the punters, with the result that pencillers were extremely hard hit. During the afternoon the Penrhiw and Maritime Colliery Brass Bands rendered pleasing selections.

Coronation Festival

At Taff Vale Park on Thursday afternoon, June 22nd 1911, there was a Coronation Festival, but in spite of many attractive features the day saw rain, and the attendance only numbered about 400. A local newspaper previewing the event wrote: -

' *The people of Pontypridd and district will on Coronation Day be afforded an opportunity of enjoying themselves in various ways at Taff Vale Park, Pontypridd. The Pontypridd Athletic Club have arranged a large and varied programme which should appeal to practically everyone inasmuch as it includes a great variety of entertainment and competitions. It is a peculiar fact to recollect that on the last Coronation Day nine years ago, the Taff Vale Park held a record crowd, in fact the numbers of people that attended on that occasion when Tom Linton endeavoured to create the World's record for the one hour's cycle riding has never since that date been exceeded, and judging by the conversation of the district it seems likely that once again a new record will be established for attendance.*

First and foremost in the programme is what is really a new institution for Pontypridd, namely, a Male Voice Competition, the first prize being offered being £20, and it seems exceedingly likely that a large number of the best choirs in Wales will compete on that popular piece "Martyrs of the Arena". There are also Ambulance Competitions open to all colliery ambulance teams and a special competition for the girls of the Red Cross Brigade.

A rustic Sports are a form of sports that have not been seen at the park for many years, and everybody attending on this occasion will have an opportunity of competing for the prizes in these various events. A large number of events are naturally included for school children, both boys and girls, and all children attending this day will be given a free Coronation souvenir. A Punch and Judy show will be provided and there will be plenty of music and dancing on the green. What, however, will probably appeal to the inhabitants of this district as being the greatest novelty will be the exhibition of what are known as daylight fireworks. The Athletic Club are going to a tremendous expense in order to get this latest form of fireworks, which are entirely new to Pontypridd. Among other things a large number of toys will be distributed among the spectators by means of these fireworks. In every way it seems as if the festival will be a great success and should especially appeal to the children of the district and owing to it being the Coronation season special arrangements have been made whereby all children will be admitted into the ground at a cost of 3d; which is a splendid reduction on this occasion.'

The various events went off without a hitch in spite of the adverse conditions. There was to have been "Dancing on the green" and fireworks, but Jupitor Plurius wouldn't allow it.

Brass Bands And School Coronation Sports

The 21st Annual Cup Competition of the Brass Bands Association was held at the Taff Vale Park on Saturday, July 2nd 1911, in the presence of a good attendance of listeners. The following Friday a Coronation Sports in connection with the Graig Council and Wood Road Catholic Schools were also held at Taff Vale Park. The older pupils, preceded by the St. Michael Home Band, marched in procession to the park where through the generosity of Councillor David Williams, excellent accommodation was afforded for the sports. Everything passed off without a hitch. Each scholar, through the kindness of the councillor, was presented with a coronation brooch or a button-hole.

Hospital Carnival - Marathon Race

In addition to the usual carnival on behalf of the Pontypridd Cottage Hospital on Friday July 13th 1911, there was a Ten Mile Marathon Race arranged by the Roath Furnishing Co. The competition started from the Workmen's Hall, Abercynon at 6.15 p.m., and was run through Cilfynydd, Coedpenmaen, Bridge Street, Taff Street and Tram Road, finishing with twenty laps (five miles) on the track at Taff Vale Park. Mr. Ted Lewis acted as starter. There were 21 entries, and out of these 19 started and 17 completed the distance, two only falling out on the way. The prizes which were all given by the Roath Furnishing Co., were awarded: - 1st, Handsome Chippendale Cabinet (or other goods) value £5-5s-0d, won by A. Edbrook, Tonyrefail, 1 hr - 10 mins; 2nd, 14 Day Marble Clock, value £3-3s-0d, won by D. Stanwick, Pontnewydd, 1 hr - 13 mins; 3rd, Eight Day Regulator Clock, value £2-2s-0d, won by E. T. Harry, Cardiff, 1 hr - 17 mins; 4th, Special prize, Pair of Bronzes, value 18s-6d, won by E. R. Price, Treharris, 1 hr - 17¼ mins.

The race caused a great amount of interest all along the route, people congregating in crowds at various vantage points to see the men go by. At Abercynon there was an immense concourse to see the start. Some amusement was caused by a man in running costume starting from Cilfynydd about a quarter of an hour before the racers, and running to the Taff Vale Park, this man bore a card on which was printed, "The R.F.C. always leads". Two of the runners gave up on the way - both being taken up by the van which followed in the rear of the men. Before the start a vote was taken as to whether the men preferred the cinder or grass track on the Taff Vale Park to run the concluding five miles, and they decided to run on the cinder track, 18 laps. Edbrook well maintained his lead the whole way and ran in good style. The heat proved very tiring, and at the conclusion of the race all the men were done up.

On Saturday the Carnival, taken altogether, was not equal to last years event. There were some exceedingly good tableaux, especially worthy mention being the American Indian Encampment and The Boy Scouts Encampment. There was again a good attendance of bands, including the Abercynon Brass Band, and the Albion, Great Western, Penrhiw and Maritime colliery bands, and Pontypridd and Ynysybwl town bands. Whilst the fancy dress judging went on, a squad from the Abercynon gymnasium gave a clever display of horse, parallel bars, and the horizontal bar, and met with considerable approval. Prizes were given for: -

Fancy Dress on horseback; Single Horse Turnout (non-business); Single Horse Turnout (trade); Colliery Underground Horse (in full working equipment); Decorated dog (led by boy or girl under 16); Fancy dress: Walking Lady, Comic Character, Decorated Cycle,

Trade Advertisement Turnout; Tableaux on Waggon; Comic Troupe or Band; Decorated Business Premises; Tug-of-war; Best Baby (under one years of age), and Best Baby (between one and two years). The Heaviest Baby in the Show prize was won by Leonard Arnold Jones, 18 months, 2st - 6lb - 12 ozs.

During the afternoon the manager of the Royal Canadian Animated Pictures, attended on the field and took a number of pictures of the chief attractions there, including the Red Cross Girls, the Scouts, and Boys and Lads Brigades going through their exercises, and then taking his position at the Municipal buildings, took films of the procession, and afterwards took films from the old bridge. These would be shown the following Monday for the benefit of the hospital funds. After the procession and later in the evening, there was a display of fireworks on the Taff Vale Park. The following week the Mill Street Schools held their second annual sports at Taff Vale Park.

August Bank Holiday Sports 1911

The chief attraction at Pontypridd over the Bank Holiday, August 6th & 7th 1911, was the excellent sports held at the Taff Vale Park, and the spectators had a rare afternoon's sport. For the 100 Yards Open Handicap alone there were well over 100 competitors. Many of the heats, the winners of which ran in the final on the following day, were keenly contested. The same remarks applied to the 300 Yards Open Handicap, in which F. C. Davies, of Tenby, was about the most popular of the heat winners. A feature of the meeting was the splendid cycling witnessed, probably about the best ever seen on the grounds. The races were productive of the greatest excitement. The Worthington Shield, which was held by Williams, of Abercwmboi, was captured after a most exciting contest by D. Hodgetts, Birmingham, D. Flynn, Glasgow, being close at his heels, and W. Kerr, Birmingham, coming in for third prize. Kerr, indeed, was exceptionally successful. He secured premier honours in the Half Mile and Two Mile Cycle Handicaps. In the Two Mile Handicap, Schneider, Champion of Australia, who was the scratch man, was responsible for a superb effort, but, though he failed to run home in his heat, he was accorded an enthusiastic ovation by the spectators. In the Half Mile Race there were four men on scratch, and one of them, D. Flynn, of Glasgow - after a fine performance came in second in the final.

The attendance on Tuesday was a little disappointing considering the ideal weather which prevailed. The foot events were evenly contested, and there were several surprises. This was the case in the final of the 100 Yards Open Handicap. Jones, of Neath, who was regarded as favourite, being well beaten by Davies, of Porth. A capital race was witnessed in the final of the 120 Yards Novice Handicap, Francis, of Llantrisant, who had done well in the heats, coming out on top by nearly a yard from R. Jones, Penydarren. The 300 Yards Flat Handicap was run in a good time, Rowe, of Pontycymmer, passing Gwyther three yards from the tape. F. C. Davies, Tenby, the back marker, put up a very fine performance in the 880 Yards Flat Handicap, and finished first with several yards to spare. The Half Mile Cycle Handicap was won by Handley, of Pontypridd, who came into the final as one of the fastest seconds in the heats, while the One Mile Scratch Race for the Professional Championship of the N.C.U. fell to Churchill, of Penygraig. The One Mile Galloway Handicap was won by C. Peters, Heolgerrig, on "Little Bess" off 290 yards.

The Welsh Powderhall Sprint 1911

The ninth Annual Welsh Sprint Handicap, otherwise known as the Welsh Powderhall, was held over Saturday and Monday 26th and 28th of August 1911 and attracted good attendance's on each afternoon. The attendance on Saturday was between 3 or 4,000, but on Monday there figures were doubled. The programme included not only the above sprint, but also a Half Mile Foot Handicap, a Half Mile and Five Mile Amateur Cycle Handicap, for all of which there were good entries of well-known athletes.

A speciality of the Half Mile Handicap on Saturday was the running of F. M. Kanley, the American Champion, and F. C. Davies, of Tenby; both men ran well and won in their heats. In the 880 Yard Foot Handicap, first prize £20, there were 53 entries, which was run

Tommy Oldfield wins 1911 Welsh Powderhall

in three preliminary heats, and the finalists for Monday were J. Walters, Bedwellty; M. Lucy, Mountain Ash; F. M. Kanley and F. C. Davies of Tenby. The Five Mile Scratch cycle Race for the South Wales N.C.U. was won by J. Hill, Cardiff.

The 130 Yards Foot Handicap, the Powderhall, first prize £100 and a gold medal; second prize £15; third, £5; and fourth, £2, was run in 16 preliminary heats, averaging six competitors in each. Each heat winner was given an award of £1. W. Thomas, of Merthyr, the winner of the medal the previous year, just succeeded in winning his heat, with Eastman, Canada, coming in as second man.

On Monday, in the Half Mile Amateur Cycle Handicap, with a first prize of £10, after four heats the final was won by V. Johnson, Birmingham. This was one of the specially good races of the day, as Johnson, who was scratch man, made a splendid run, passing each of his fellows, and won easily by about three lengths. The 300 Yards Foot Handicap was won by Ivor James, 26 Yds, of Merthyr. In the final of the 880 Yards Foot Handicap, Walters, who was the limit man, maintained a lead throughout and won rather comfortably, though his lead was gradually being diminished by the American, Kanley, and the finish for second place between him and Lucy was very exciting, and the latter only succeeded almost on the tape.

After the four semi-final heats of the Welsh Sprint, at last it was time for the final. As a result of the heats it was apparent that the final would be a grand contest, and this it really proved to be, for never since the introduction of this race had there been such an extremely close finish. The four men, Goldsmith of London; Oldfield, Cardiff; Rees, Glanaman; and Rowe, Pontycymmer, kept their relative positions well until half the course had been covered. From this point onward it was seen that the honours of the day lay with Oldfield and Rowe. The latter had a start of three yards over his rival, and he appeared to maintain it for nearly 100 yards. It was at this stage that Oldfield, who ran very strongly throughout, was gaining on Rowe. For another two or three yards they were all but abreast, though Rowe had slightly the advantage. This position was maintained almost until the tape was reached, and it was this which probably accounted for the impression that it was Rowe that had won. A great number of the crowd were convinced that this was so until Oldfield's number was put up. And this was the signal for a remarkable outburst. Booing and cries of dissent were loudly indulged in. The hostility to the decision was by no means directed against Oldfield personally, as was evidence by the fact that no demonstration of antagonism was shown him on his way to the dressing-room. The dissatisfaction was confined more particularly to those in the vicinity of the grandstand, who were in a better position to see than those in other parts of the field. On the other hand, it must be conceded that the officials who were on the spot were far better able to judge than those in the field, however well placed. As a matter of fact, so close together were the two men that it was really only those on the tape who could decide the issue with any degree of accuracy, and the Pontypridd Athletic Club officials must be credited with absolute honesty. It is also noteworthy that Rowe himself did not raise any objection to the decision, and there can be no doubt whatever as to who had won. Result of 1911 Welsh Powderhall: 1st. Tommy Oldfield, 9½ Yds, Cardiff; 2nd. Alec Rowe, 12½ Yds, Pontycymmer; 3rd. R. O. Rees, 8 Yds, Glannamman; 4th. F. G. Goldsmith, 5 Yds, London. A snapshot of the finish was taken by Mr. A. O. Forrest, Market Square.

Dragons At Taff Park

On September 4th 1911 the new Pontypridd Association Club, nicknamed "The Dragons" , opened their career with a friendly home game against Queens Park Rangers at Taff Vale Park. Although defeated 1-2 by a team that included several players who had played league football, a crowd of around 4,000 spectators watched the game. The early days, however, were not entirely free of trouble and the Glamorgan Free Press of November 17th 1911 wrote: -

' *Pontypridd met Aberdare for the third time in a Welsh Cup tie on Saturday, and won by 1-0. It will be remembered that the first meeting, at Aberdare. ended in a 2-2 draw. The replay at Taff Vale Park resulted in a victory 1-0 for the dragons; but Aberdare protested against the result on the grounds of 1. That the goal was not a legitimate one, and 2. That the close proximity of the cycle track to the touchline made the ground dangerous and unfit for a cup-tie. On the first point the protest failed, but the second claim was upheld and a replay was ordered at Penydarren Park, Merthyr, on Saturday, November 18th.'*

1912

The Glamorgan Free Press of April 5th 1912 wrote: -

Dragons Great Victory - Huge Crowd At Taff Vale Park

'Pontypridd and Cardiff City are to meet for the Welsh Cup at Ninian Park on Easter Monday! That is the momentous fact which has sent every follower of soccer in Pontypridd into wild hysterics of delight. Let me start at the beginning. There has never been such a crowd at Taff Vale Park before. It must have numbered about 8,000; and the scene just before the kick-off must have buoyed up the hearts of the Pontypridd directors. The mascots duly made their appearance - Ton's bull-dog and Ponty's white pomeranian - and so did the two bands, which in turn sent martial strains quivering into space. On every branch of the trees skirting the river-side, daring men and boys had perched themselves and hundreds had squatted themselves on the slopes of the embankment on the other side of the river, from whence the obtained a good view of the game without paying! All of a sudden the Dragon's lilting war song burst from fifty lusty throats from the Cardiff end of the ground and out came the Dragons. They had a rousing reception; so did Ton Pentre, who followed them, for they had brought hundreds of lusty-lunged supporters. '

The match itself, on a Thursday, saw the Dragons win this Semi-final of the Welsh cup, and was all the more remarkable because of the sudden and dramatic transformation that the game underwent in the last quarter of an hour. Up to fifteen minutes off the end the Rhonddaites were leading by 1-0, and the Pontypridd forwards had so far shown such indifferent form that their supporters were despairing of their even equalising. Then in a twinkling, the wily Dragons made a terrific rally that made every heart throb with excitement, and scoring three goals in ten minutes, ran out winners 3-1, and now faced Cardiff City in the final. The thousands of Dragons supporters were overjoyed to think that a club which only came into existence at the beginning of the season should have got to the final of the Welsh Cup. The final, at Ninian Park before 18,000 spectators, saw a 0-0 draw, the home goalkeeper saving a penalty. The replay at Aberdare on April 18th, saw the Dragons defeated 3-0.

Whitsun 1912

For the first time since 1903, due to the Dragons playing home there was no Easter athletic meeting at Taff Vale Park. However, the honours at Taff Vale Park on Whit-Monday 1912 fell to W. Murray, of Birmingham, who accomplished the notable achievement of being the first in the final of three separate events - the Half-mile and Two-mile Cycle Handicap and the One Mile Scratch Cycle Race - the last named event, however, was declared a "no-race" as a consequence upon the time limit having been exceeded. D. Hodgetts, the holder of the title of the Worthington Shield arrived too late to defend his title. Hodgetts had motored up from Carmarthen, but his motor broke down on the way to Pontypridd. However, as the race was declared void, he remained holder of the shield!

Monday proved an ideal day of outdoor amusements, and as a consequence some 4,000 people had assembled, but Tuesday was not so good, with the result that the attendance was not so large. The outstanding performer of the afternoon's sport being Reg Walker, the celebrated South African "Crack" and ex-amateur world champion sprinter. Aided by a good wind, and with the track in excellent condition, Walker's capital running in his earlier efforts was deservedly applauded, but when in the 130 Yards Open Handicap he got away from scratch in the semi-final, and did the distance in 12.15 seconds - eight yards inside evens - and just better than the worlds previous best, and he received a tremendous ovation. In the final which, fell to Walker after a magnificent race, the colonial's time was 12.25 secs. Holway, the American sprinter, who had put up so many fine performances at Taff Vale Park, was again amongst the competitors, but was unfortunate in being drawn against S. J.

Thomas, of Aberaman, on the good mark of 18 yards and the scratch man was beaten by a couple of inches. There was also a 100 Yards Footballers Race, with 15 entries, which was won by A. Stone, Pontypridd. The 120 Yards Novice Handicap, which had 56 entries, was won by L. Furber, Pontypridd; whilst the 120 Yards Open Handicap by the aforementioned S. J. Thomas. There were 41 entries for the 150 Yards Whippet Race, which saw "Ramble" belonging to J. Williams, Bargoed, come first.

South African Crack Beaten

An attractive programme of professional athletics and amateur cycling events were presented at the Taff Vale Park on Monday and Wednesday July 29th and 31st 1912. Chief interest was created in the reappearance of Walker, the S. African crack, who had won a big sprint at Manchester the previous Saturday. He competed in the 120 Yards Open Foot Handicap, off scratch, but lost his heat to a local man by a yard. The Half Mile Cycle Championship provided an exciting finish, Newman, Penygraig, winning from J. Hill, Cardiff, by inches.

Tuesdays events were postponed owing to the weather, and on Wednesday, despite fine weather, the attendance was not up to expectations. The 120 Yards Open Foot Handicap proved a capital race, the first three competitors finishing close up, Trevor Williams, Pontypridd, winning from G. Williams, Taffs Well, with G. Rees, Merthyr, fourth. Judge, of Llantwit, who was the favourite, won the novice sprint in fine style. The Half Mile Foot Handicap was won by F. C. Davies, Tenby, who was the back marker, with over a yard to spare. A notable victory was that gained by Harry Cullum, the Cardiff veteran, in the One Mile Race. The Mile and a Half Trotting Handicap was won by "Little Dolly" of Merthyr off 390 yards.

The 1912 £140 Welsh Powderhall

There was a notable gathering of the world's crack sprinters for the 1912 Powderhall over August 24th and 26th, which was held a week earlier than usual due to the soccer season, including Walker, South Africa; Postle, Donaldson and Shaw, Australia; Eastman, Canada;

Holway, America, and Goldsmith, London. An interesting entry was that of bombardier Wells the English Heavy-weight Boxing Champion, who was a good runner and had appeared on the cinder track on many occasions. Vigrollie, of Paris, one of the best professional sprinters in France also made his first appearance in South Wales, and his countryman, Montellier, took part in the Mile and Half Mile Handicap. Previous winners of the Welsh Sprint taking part were Holway, Oldfield, W. Thomas, Merthyr; and C. Evans, Tenby. From a numerical point of view there were 118 entries, 93 being accepted. In the heats on Saturday before 4,000 spectators, all the previous winners and Wells, failed to survive the heats. The best times were returned by M. J. Crowley, Cardiff; E. M. Williams, Hopkinstown; S. J. Thomas, Aberaman; and J. Davies, Bargoed. The draw for the semi-finals resulted in all the crack men being placed in different heats, so that another afternoon's interesting sport was promised for Monday. The Monday crowd was double of that on Saturday. In the big sprint final Crowley, off 16 yards, won by about a yard from Davies, 12 yards, with Hall, Clydach, third, and Stoddart, Penygraig, fourth. J. Crowley was 22 years of age and had played for Cardiff Rugby club reserves the previous winter, but stated that he intended joining Pontypridd in the coming rugby season.

Annual Hospital Carnival

The third Annual Carnival and Sports for the Pontypridd Cottage Hospital was held on August 29th 1912 at the Taff Vale Park, but the weather was unfavourable and a counter-attraction, which included the appearance of an aeroplane, at Caerphilly, and the people of Trehafod and Hopkinstown having already held its own event the previous day, seriously distracted from the number of spectators.

Scene At Dragons Game

A serious incident happened when the Pontypridd Dragons faced Llanelly before 4 to 5,000 spectators at Taff Vale Park on September 5th 1912. The game was a rough one throughout, the Dragons seemingly being the only side to be on the receiving end of a large number of injuries. Llanelly were leading 2-1, when towards the close the Llanelly forwards, who had earlier missed a penalty, were going great guns, and it was during one of these furious onslaughts that a sensational incident happened. Turner, the Pontypridd goalkeeper, had cleared with a cluster of players around him, when Peters, the Llanelly centre-forward, deliberately kicked him. With a sharp "Oh!" the Dragons' popular goalkeeper fell on his back and writhed in pain, but it was all in pretence, for when Dalton sharply told him to get up he immediately sprang to his feet and assumed a threatening attitude. Members of both teams swarmed round him and the situation looked very ugly till the referee, having with others attended to Turner, ordered him off the field for his cowardly action. With a look of concern he proceeded towards the pavilion. Immediately there was a rush on the part of spectators towards the entrance, and the offending player found "the way out" completely blocked by the crowd, who expressed their opinion of him in no unmeasured terms. There he stood, "thinking his thoughts" while the crowd hurled their anathemas at him. Lucky for him they were the "season ticket" folk and "shillingites", for his action had kindled such indignation in the minds of the whole of the spectators that hundreds of them would not have been able to restrain themselves if he had been within reach of them. Taking in the situation the referee stopped the game while some officials attempted to clear a way for the "footballer". The crowds surged round him as he tried to force his way through them, and trembling hearts expected something exciting to happen at any moment. Eventually they managed to get him to the dressing room, and the game proceeded. Peters had no sooner left the ground than the Dragons obtained the equaliser, and saved the match. The result of 2-2, saw gate takings of £84.

1913

Dragons £350 Gate - Record Takings

On March 8th 1913, the Pontypridd Dragons association team defeated Chester 2-1 at Wrexham in the semi-final of the Welsh cup, securing a second consecutive cup final appearance. On Easter Monday, March 31st, the record sum of £350 was taken at the Taff

Vale Park in a Southern league match between the Dragons and Cardiff City. This was all the more remarkable because nothing depended on the result, Cardiff having already secured promotion from division two, and the Dragons having no chance of honours in that direction. However, the interest caused by the Dragons reaching the Welsh Cup final had created quite an interest. The Dragons director's decision to have a shilling gate instead of the normal 6d was thoroughly justified. Owing to the wretched weather just before and after Christmas the club had suffered greatly, and it was felt that football enthusiasts in the district would not object to parting with an extra "tanner" under the circumstances, especially with such attractive opponents on view such as Cardiff City, the prospective champions. People ought to have been grateful to the promoters of the club in Pontypridd, who have enabled them to witness football of a very good class at Taff Vale Park and ought to be glad of helping the club. They DID seize this opportunity on Monday, when they willingly parted with a shilling, and the directors, at the head of whom was that popular sportsman, County Councillor David Williams, thanked them for their generous attitude. The gate would help provide summer wages for the players. The crowd numbered 7,500.

It was quite an ideal day for football and the ground was in good condition, and the holiday crowd was in a most merry mood. The gates were opened an hour before the kick-off time - 3.30 - and from the outset there was a steady flow of spectators, who freely sported the colours of their respective teams. The Dragons supporters, of course, predominated, but the Welsh metropolitans brought train-loads of followers with them, and they undoubtedly made their presence felt. Several excursions were run from Cardiff, including a new route via the Rhymney Railway, through Caerphilly. The Dragons were determined to make a great effort to lower the colours of the champions, and not one Dragon player spared himself, and the excitement towards the end was intense, although it had been a dour struggle that ended 0-0, but if the Dragons had snatched a win - which they almost did - what a scene there would have been. In spite of the keenness it was a very clean match. There was no Easter or Whitsun athletic sports meeting again this year due to the Dragons fixture list. On April 18th 1913 the Dragons drew 0-0 at the Welsh Cup final with Swansea at Ninian Park, Cardiff, before a crowd of 8,310, Pontypridd missing a penalty. The replay took place at the Mid-Rhondda ground on Thursday, April 24th, when Swansea won 1-0. The Dragons received a share of the £463 taken on the gate over the two games.

Tournament In Aid Of Cottage Hospital

On Saturday July 12th 1913 a Military Tournament and Ambulance Competition in aid of the Cottage Hospital was held at Taff Vale Park. The idea of the tournament was first mooted by the Hon. secretary, Mr. G. Williams, who considered that the usual carnival was getting a bit stale, and it was therefore necessary to have some novelty, or the hospital would not be successful in obtaining anything like the sum obtained in former years. The tournament proved a success and as a result the hospital would now receive £100, and the Athletic Club deserved thanks for not only having lent the Taff Vale Park, but also for the lot of work that they carried out in order to make the ground usable by this date.

August Bank Holiday 1913

The members of the Pontypridd Athletic Club were to be congratulated on making such extensive improvements at Taff Vale Park, such as making it one of the best trotting grounds in South Wales; secondly they deserved the thanks of the sporting public for providing another good two-day meeting. The old cycle track had been done away with, and with the additional ground, the space had been made into a fine track for Galloway racing. The foot events were still held in the centre of the park as previously. On Monday the crowd was about 2,000 and there was also a large crowd on Tuesday. Events were: - 120 Yards Novice Handicap (71 entries); 120 Yards Open Handicap (79 entries); 330 Yards Open Handicap (52 entries); 880 Yards Open Handicap; 1½ Mile Trotting Handicap (16 entries); 1 Mile Trotting Handicap (16 entries) and 150 Yards Whippet Handicap (53 Entries).

Pontypridd Dragons at T.V. Park, Circa 1913

During the summer of 1913 the Dragons committee were working on Taff Vale Park. The Glamorgan Free Press of August 28th reported: - *'The enclosure is being suitably terraced, crush barriers will be erected which will add considerably to the comfort of the spectators, and arrangements made so that all that enter the grounds have a good view of the matches. '*

Welsh Powderhall 1913

From the reception accorded to the 11th Annual Welsh Powderhall at the Taff Vale Park, it would seem that the great footrace of the year was steadily increasing in public favour. There were fully 6,500 spectators present, and the promoters were to be congratulated on the excellence of the sports provided. The programme on Saturday was a long one, as in addition to the heats of the sprint, there was a Half Mile Handicap and a 1½ Mile Galloway Handicap. Amongst the acceptances for the big sprint this year, which constituted a record, numbering over 100, were Jack Donaldson, (World Champion); Carter, Shaw and Newbury, Australia; and these all put in appearance, but unfortunately B. R. Day, Blackpool, and Bombardier Wells were absent. As in previous occasions there were several surprise results in the preliminary heats and this could be accounted for by the favourable weather which prevailed all the afternoon, and in the condition of the track. Crowley, Cardiff, who was last years winner; H. M. Davies, winner of the recent Cardiff Stadium Sprint; Williams, who won the Cambrian Dash, and Carter, Australia, were all beaten in their heats. The favourite, W. P. Thomas, the Pontypridd and Cardiff rugby threequarter, off 18½ yards, not only held his lead in his heat, but increased it, and this while running well within himself. Burgess, of Pontypridd, proved another popular winner, winning some inches in front of Williams. Donaldson, who met with a most flattering reception, ran splendidly. The Half Mile Open Handicap was won by Williams, Taff Well, while the 1½ Mile Galloway Handicap was won by B. Mitchell, Llantwit Fardre.

Over 7,000 passed through the turnstiles to witness the semi-finals and final of the Powderhall on Monday. In addition to these there was a One-mile Flat Handicap with a large entry and substantial prizes, a 1½ Mile Trotting Handicap, and a 300 Yards Open Flat Handicap, also with a big entry, truly a programme to suit all, and a good three hours sports, and the events were run well to time. The favourite for the coveted Powderhall £100 and a gold medal, given by Mr. Morgan Evans, of the Sportsman Hotel, was W. P. Thomas, a young Pontypriddian, but he was well beaten in the semi-final round by J. Helens, the young Newcastle runner, who proved to be the ultimate winner. F. C. Davies, Cardiff, was made firm favourite for the first heat, and justified the confidence by winning very easily. The second heat saw Jack Donaldson make a great effort. He seemed to have too much to do fifty yards from the tape, but to the great delight of the huge crowd he just got up, and won by an "eyelash" so to speak. The third heat was the one won by Helens. In the last of the heats punters again had a set-back, as Burgess upset a well supported Hall, Clydach, winning by half a yard. On the watch Helens looked a good thing for the final.

At the start of the final in silence the men got down in the holes, and with an excellent start they were sent away. It was evident, after the half distance had been covered, that the favourite was, unless something unforeseen happened, bound to win and this he did in no half-hearted fashion, winning comfortably by a yard and a half. He had accomplished a capital performance, and had never given his backers any cause for uneasiness. He had been well supported, and his party looked mighty pleased when seen immediately after he had undergone the usual camera performance. The result of the 1913 Welsh Powderhall was: 1st, J. Helens, Newcastle, 15 Yds; 2. F. C. Davies, Cardiff, 13 Yds; 3. C. R. Burgess, Pontypridd, 17 Yds; J. Donaldson, Australia, Scratch.

The One Mile Flat Handicap was won by D. E. Emmanuel, Ogmore Vale off 155 yards start, while the 1½ Mile Trotting Handicap, after five heats, saw the final won by "Pengam Lad" owned by J. Simons, Pengam. The second round of the 300 Yards Open Flat Handicap was run in seven heats of twelve entries, and was won in the final by J. Harris, Abergwynfi off 36 yards.

On October 27th 1913, a thunderstorm occurred in the district, and a cyclone was formed in the valley, leaving two dead. Fencing at Taff Vale Park was blown down and sheets of iron were thrown in the air like aeroplanes to the other side of the river.

1914

On May 16th 1914, the first of a series of athletic meetings was successfully conducted at the Taff Vale Park, with a 120 Yards Flat Handicap, the final being won by J. E. Powell, Cardiff, and a 150 Yards Whippet Handicap, which after 12 heats saw the final won by Mr. A. Woods's "Fussy" off 28 Yards.

Whitsun 1914

Two splendid athletic programmes were gone through at the Taff Vale Park on Whit-Monday and Tuesday, 3rd & 4th June, 1914. The fixture was so well patronised that the attendance on Monday was above the average for Whit-Monday gatherings. Monday's meeting was devoted to the foot and horse racing. The latter was growing in popularity with the crowd, and the number of entries in both ensured a fine holiday treat. Although somewhat cloudy during the greater part of the day, it did not rain. One of the features of Monday's events was the running of L. Furber, a local athlete, who carried off the prizes for the two foot events. He showed splendid form throughout, but he only won one final by fortune, as this provided a close event, only inches dividing the first three. There was also an exciting finish in the final of the Galloway, in which interest was sustained until the last moment. "Little Tom" won a great race.

On the second day, although the attendance was good, it was not exactly of the dimensions which the programme merited. The sport provided was of a high order, and the foot events captured the chief interest. Each of these events was well contested. The fixture, however, was not without its surprises, for E. M. Williams, a local sprinter, won the 120 Yards Open Handicap, while Len Judge, the popular Pontypridd Rugbyite came second in three events. The 300 Yards Handicap was won by D. O. Davies, Ferndale. Here the finish was very close, and F. C. Davies of Cardiff, who had previously figured at the park, made a splendid effort to get placed. The Half Mile Handicap was won comfortably by Porter, now of Swindon, and an old Newport amateur. The additional feature on Tuesday, were the Tug-of-war competitions and Whippet Handicaps. In the former Cwmdare 'A' beat Pentre. The eight-man competition attracted much interest; indeed, the pulls occasionally raised the spectators to the tip-toe of excitement. The 150 Yards Whippet Handicap was won by J. Whiles's "Bloomer", J. T. Evans, Ystrad, won the 120 Yards Novice Handicap. On Monday June 29th there were more Galloway and Trotting Races.

August Bank Holiday 1914

The August bank holiday sports organised by the Pontypridd Athletic Club which took place at Taff Vale Park on Monday August 1st 1914 was very well patronised. The entries numbering 400 were well above the average and a capital afternoon's sport was provided. Chief interest was centred in the sprint handicaps in view of the Welsh Powderhall which was to be held shortly at the park. Several well known sprinters participated in various events. Len Judge, a Pontypridd R.F.C. footballer, won the Novice Sprint and also entered the final of the Open Handicap. W. P. Thomas, another well known runner competed in the 300 Yards and would have won his heat easily but for the fact that in looking back three or four yards from the tape he slipped and fell. This was rather unfortunate as he was a very strong favourite for the final. R. G. Williams, of Pontypridd, who showed capital form, won the 120 Yards Open Handicap after a very fine race. Another local man T. Morgan came second, the third going to a Barry competitor. E. M. Williams, Pontypridd, also won the 300 Yards Flat Handicap, winning from F. C. Davies, the famous Cardiff and Tenby pedestrian. There was also a 120 Yards Boys Race, won by S. Baker, Pontypridd, a 150 Yards Whippet Handicap, won by Mr. R. Rees's "Jane", and a 880 Yards Flat Handicap, won by D. Jones, Onllwyn.

The officials were as follows: Judges: Messrs. Ack Llewellin, Fred Morris and John Phillips. Treasurer, Mr. David Williams; Starter, Mr. Ted Lewis; Marksman, Mr. E. Johns. Handicappers: Foot, Mr.

Ted Lewis; Whippet, Mr. John Doran; Timekeeper and referee, Mr. Fred Morris. The club committee: Dr. Howard Davies, Chairman; Messrs. Ack Llewellin, Ivor Howell, J. Williams, J. Phillips, A. Amos, D. Williams, T. Griffiths, S. Barkaway, G. Barkaway.

Welsh Powderhall 1914

By the date of the 1914 Welsh Powderhall, war against Germany had already broken out, but the event was still held, though several competitors did not appear on the day, probably having already joined the armed forces. The Glamorgan Free Press carried this report: -

'The question elsewhere is asked, "how should we comfort ourselves, during the war?" The answer - the only answer - is, "as men, and not as weaklings." Surely, there is no reason why we should walk about in sackcloth and aches, or slacken normal activities. Our recreations must go on, as well as our duties, and it interesting to note that the twelfth annual Welsh Sprint Handicap on Saturday and Monday, August 29th and 31st, promises to be as attractive as ever, in spite of the fact that the public mind is more or less concentrated upon the war. The entries, numerically, showed a slight falling off, though of quality they were much superior. The famous competitors comprised the winner of the Cambrian Dash, T.J. Hughes, Abertillery, and R. Seymour, Bingley, winner of the Cardiff Stadium £100 Handicap. Bombadier Wells, British Heavyweight Champion, was a certain starter. The formidable seven-stone boxer of the world, Jimmy Wilde, known as the "Might atom" and the "Tylorstown Terror" entered the Half Mile Handicap. Wilde was purposed to train under Benny Williams of Llantwit Major. There would have been many more popular entries but for the fact that the committee felt duty bound to carry out the programme as advertised. Once the starters were publicised, they could not accept further entries. The event diverted public attention from the incessant war babble, and for that they were indebted to the promoters, who, distinguished in the realm of sport, had spared no effort to accomplish an unprecedented success in this very eventful and historic year. '

In many respects the meeting was a memorable one. A striking feature was the success of the local pedestrians. None of the English "cracks" qualified for the second round. Donaldson together with the Manchester and Sheffield representatives, being defeated in their respective heats, whilst Helens, Newcastle, last years winner, did not put in an appearance. For once in was a purely Welsh final. Pontypridd had no less than three representatives in the second round, but only one, W. P. Thomas reached the final stage. Footballers were to the fore. Joe Jones, Treorchy, and Len Judge, Pontypridd ; Dai Evans, Blaenclydach; and W. P. Thomas, Pontypridd, all took a prominent part in the popular winter pastime.

The final produced a very exciting race. W. P. Thomas, 18 Yards, actually took the lead, but he failed to maintain the pace, and gave way to Andrews, Cardiff, 19 Yards, who reached the tape a yard ahead of Quant of Merthyr, 19½ Yards, Andrews, who was the favourite from the start, in each of his heats was odds on winning, was the winner, with Quant second, D. Evans, 18 Yards, 3rd, and W. P. Thomas, fourth.

The Athletic Syndicate were also to be congratulated upon securing the entries of some of the best horses in the country. On Saturday Mr. S. Williams, Swansea, had two horses, one of which, "The Belle", carried off the prize in the 1½ Mile Trotting Galloway. On Monday the trotting was much appreciated by the crowd, and it was clear that the public was keen upon more of these events being introduced. However, the military situation would take first priority, and this was the last Athletic meeting at Taff Vale Park for four years. The weekly sports events that had begun in 1902 were now a firm feature of the British athletics scene, mainly thanks to David Williams and Teddy Lewis, who seemed to be the driving force behind the committee. However, since the Dragons soccer team had taken out a lease, the athletics seem to have had part of its season curtailed due to the pitch being needed, and the big Easter meetings were now a thing of the past. What sort of effect would the war have on the population; how long would it last; and would the people return to Taff Vale Park when the war was over?

Chapter Five 1915 - 1920

Despite the war there were still minor sports events at T.V. Park, but these all seem to come to an end after a year when the Pontypridd Observer of May 1st 1915 commented: *'But for Councillor David Williams there would be very little sport in Pontypridd. The "Syndicate", of which he is head, controlling events on the park have, however, definitely decided that it is not advisable to get up a programme for Whitsun.'* It seems very little happened after this statement, but a Scouts Drum Head service was held at T.V. Park on Sunday, May 9th 1915, when troops from Berw Rd, Treforest, Porth, Mid-Rhondda, Penygraig and Dinas attended. The service was conducted by Mr. D. Davies, Treforest, who delivered a short address on "fight the good fight". Appropriate hymns were sung, concluding with the national anthem. The lads were entertained to tea by the Treforest troop.

Rugby and Soccer Benefit Football Matches

A rugby match between a Pontypridd / Cardiff (W. P. Thomas) XV and Pontypool (Welsh Champions) was played on Taff Vale Park on Saturday, May 13th 1916, in aid of the Pontypridd Cottage Hospital. Shepherd, Mountain Ash, scored an unconverted try for the home side in the first half. In the second half Rhys Harry equalised for Pontypool, the game ending in a 3-3 draw. Admission was 6d and 1s. For the following two years Taff Vale Park seems to have been devoid of anything of note until in the first week in April 1918 when a charity football match, East v West was held there with the ground in excellent fettle, with the turf fine and springy. A splendid holiday crowd attended and despite the attention of Jupitor Plurius, midway, the dexterity with which the ball was manipulated often grew applause from the appreciative spectators. East beat West by six goals to nothing. The Great Western Colliery Silver Band discoursed sweet strains of enchanting music and the excellent way in which they played for forty-five minutes before the game started as well as when marching to and from the ground, showed the generous way in which this assistance was given. The balls, given by local shopkeepers, Messrs P. Lougher and S .Wiltshire, were both used, and were sent to France to be played with out there by Capt Seaton's Boys. As a result of the game it was anticipated that about £90 would be sent to Capt. Seaton by the organiser, Councillor David Williams.

Whippet racing on a small scale seemed to continue at Taff Vale Park throughout the war, though few were reported until 1918 when meetings again were covered in the local newspapers. One such meeting took place on Saturday, June 15th 1918, when a successful sports were held under the auspices of the S. Wales and Mon. Whippet Association. A series of Boys' races and whippet events took place. The weather was ideal and the historic running grounds brought back memories of many famous runners. There was an excellent entry of 128 whippets and 60 boys, the racing being very interesting.

1918 also saw a return of other events to Taff Vale Park, one of the first was on Thursday, August 15th 1918 when a successful sports and baby show were held under the auspices of the Treforest and District Allotment Society. The baby show was a record, there being 60 entries. The results were as follows: - Baby Under 6 Months Old, winner, Phillip Martin, 69 The Parade, Pontypridd; Over 6 Months and Under 12 Months, winner, William Smart, 6 River St, Trehafod; Over One Year and Under Two Years, winner Morfydd Howells, 8 Windsor Rd, who was also voted best baby in show. The president, Mr. D. L. Davies J. P; President of the Pontypridd Urban District Council, said that the competition had been very keen as all the children who were entered were exceedingly well fed and this reflected much credit on their parents. There was a very large number of entries in the sports and the various events were keenly contested. The Judges were Councillor David Williams (Greyhound Hotel) and Mr. Denis Thomas (Bridge Hotel). The events were: 80 Yards Boys' Race; 80 Yards Allotment Holders Race, men over 40 years of age; Tug-of-war; and a Ladies Race. There was various side shows. A flower stall was well patronised. The whole of the proceeds were in aid of the Pontypridd Cottage Hospital.

Another early event near the end of the war that took place on Taff Vale Park was a Grand Rustic Sports, which was held on Saturday, August 31st 1918 in connection with the Pontypridd and District Federated Allotment Association. There was a Tug-of-war championship, Boy Scouts Display and Baby show. There was dancing on the green, and music once again by the Great Western Colliery Silver Band. There were excellent side shows, including - Bomb the Kaiser, Prowling Cats, Kicking Donkey, Etc; Etc. Admission was 6d (Tax Extra).

The 6th Volunteer Battalion of the Welsh Regiment held a Battalion Parade and Annual Inspection at Taff Vale Park at 9.45 a.m., Sunday, October 27th 1918. A special train was run from Treherbert at 1 p.m. and returned at 4 p.m.

1919

The end of the great war saw regular sports quickly returned to Taff Vale Park, starting with a £12-10s Whippet Handicap on Monday April 24th 1919, there being over 120 entries, and April 27th saw a galloway and whippet meeting.

Gates Rushed at Dragons match

The Dragons soccer club hit trouble in their first home match of the season on March 8th 1919 when Cardiff City were the visitors. The weather was fine, but owing to bad arrangements at the entrance to the ground, there were at least 200 to 300 persons who gained admission without payment by rushing the gate. The crush was so great, that there seemed there would be a serious accident, but fortunately, nothing serious occurred, only the loss to the coffers of the club. The attendance appeared to be about 5,000, and after a scoreless first half, the Dragons ran out eventual winners by 3-0.

On May 3rd 1919 there was a sports event which included a 100 Yards Open Handicap, won by Charlie Pitman, Pontypridd, plus a 100 Yards Boys Handicap, Baby show, and other sports in aid of the St John's Ambulance (Pontypridd) War Memorial Fund. Later in May, on the 24th, Cardiff City ladies played a soccer match against the Pontypridd discharged soldiers. Monday May 25th 1919 saw the

Australian sprinter Jack Donaldson and C. J. Mears race a 100 Yards Sprint at Taff Vale Park for £100. Mears, the favourite, maintained a slight lead from the start and won by a foot. Other events were: 120 Yards Handicap; 880 Yards Handicap, 150 Yards Whippet Race and a One Mile Gallop.

June 21st 1919 saw a Fancy Dress Carnival and Sports held under the auspices of the St. John's Church, Graig, in aid of the War Memorial Fund . In the first week in July the Pontypridd Police played St. John's Guild at cricket at Taff Vale Park, and on July 23rd the Pontypridd Police played the Glamorgan County Police, losing by 27 runs. On August 4th and 6th there were more sports, and a large crowd witnessed athletics, trotting, cycling and whippet racing.

Welsh Powderhall 1919

Judging by the attendance at the Taff Vale Park on both Saturday and Monday, August 30th and September 1st 1919, the Welsh Powderhall had not ceased to be attractive in spite of the lapse of four years due to the war. Most of the best known runners in South Wales, and a few from the different parts of England and Scotland, competed in the big event, the entries eclipsing all previous records. In all, twenty heats were necessary to decide who were to appear in the final stages on Monday, and the handicapping resulted in some keen contests. As there had been very little racing over the 130 yards distance since the outbreak of war, and with so many new men in the field, the issue was regarded as very open. There were, however. few, if any, surprises. A. Jenkins, Rhydyfelin and T. Gregory, Port Talbot, who were the strong favourites, won their heats in comfortable fashion. J. H. Thomas, Pembroke Dock; E. N. Price, Cardiff; Reynolds, Caerphilly., and F. Lawless, Eastleigh, all ran well, particularly the latter. On Saturday, the two scratch horses in the One Mile Galloway Handicap - "Miss Ethel" and "Princess Pat" - both fell in their respective heats, and the rider of the former, a boy named Will Humphreys, was badly shaken. The event was won by Mr. Schofield's (Pontypridd) "Toby 2". The Three Lap Galloway was won by Mr. King's "fairyland".

After a very fine race on Monday, F. Lawless, Eastleigh, won the Welsh Powderhall. The feature of the handicap was the prominent running of the South Wales runners. The surprise of the Semi-final was the defeat of Gregory, who was strongly fancied to win outright. Result of the 1919 Welsh Powderhall: 1st F. Lawless, 14½ Yds; 2nd. B. Williams, 11½ Yds, Llanelly; 3rd. A. Jenkins, 18 Yds, Rhydyfelin; 4th. W. A. Jones, 15½ Yds, Neath Abbey.

There were also the finals of the 300 Yards Handicap; One Mile Trotting Handicap, ¾ Mile Galloway, and Three Laps Trotting. Meanwhile, on Tuesday the Dragons soccer club held a trial match at Taff Vale Park.

1920

Cup Finalists At Taff Vale Park

Weather typical of March prevailed at Taff Vale Park on April 20th 1920, when Aston Villa in compliance with the transfer of H. Nash, sent down practically a full team. About 2,000 persons witnessed a game which was robbed of interesting features by the state of the greasy ground, the strong wind, and bitterly cold rain. In the first half Read and A. Davies scored from good shots, and Boyman negotiated the next from a penalty, to leave the visitors leading 3-0 at half-time. In the second half Rampton, A. Evans and Parks equalised for the Dragons. Five minutes from the close a penalty was given against the Dragons, from which Boyman scored, and a minute later Humphries put on the fifth goal, leaving Aston Villa winners 5-3. A week later the same Aston Villa team played in the F.A. Cup Final at Wembley!

On May the 1st 1920, Athletic Sports and Whippet Racing took place at the park, and the concluding heats in the 150 Yards Whippet Handicap for £20 produced a remarkable final, "White Squall", 15½ Yards, owned by Mr. Jones, Mountain Ash, and "Ragtime Hero", 17½ Yards, owned by Mr. Jones, Wattstown, two brother dogs, making a dead heat on two occasions. At the third attempt "White Squall" won by a foot. At the same meeting an 80 Yards Boys Handicap was won by Tommy Davies, Pontypridd.

Dragons Take up Lease

At a meeting of the Dragons supporters club in late May 1920, the chairman, Mr. E. R. Rogers, in a speech apologised to the members that there had been a long delay in placing the terms of the acquisition of Taff Vale Park before them. The club had first negotiated to get the ground, but they could come to no agreement. They were not in a position to purchase the ground and so they had to raise fresh capital to lease it. Eventually, he himself took the responsibility of leasing the ground; the ground and the purchase was now being completed. The terms assured the football club of whatever lease they wish to take up. He was in an awkward position. He was a member of the syndicate and a director of the club. As far as they had gone the ground had been purchased, but it was impossible for him to say anything on the question of returns. He appealed to every member of the supporters club to get two or three friends to join the club. They needed a great deal of money and he could say that the ground cost £5,000. He wanted the supporters to have a strong hand in the control of the football club and the only way to get that was by getting an increase in membership of the supporters club and to buy shares, and so get the controlling interest and responsibility they were entitled to. He was going to get some of the business men in the town to give their support to the club. He was sorry that that so few businessmen in the town took interest in the football club. The football clubs patronised the shops and amusements in the middle of the town and he was of the opinion that those who benefited in that way should support the club in return. The members of the supporters club numbered 250, and he looked forward to the time when it would number 2,500. Mr. J. T. Morgan, another supporters' representative on the board of directors, said that he was quite satisfied with the progress of the supporters club that was formed in September 1919, and had purchased 290 shares in the club. A week or two after Whitsun help would be required down at Taff Vale Park to remove the track and he appealed to all present to go down and do what they could to help. In this way they could save the club about £100.

The following item appeared in the Pontypridd Observer on July 3rd 1920: - Taff Vale Park (Pontypridd) Co. Ltd - Private Company. Capital £5,000 in £1 shares. To provide grounds and premises for Cricket, Football, Bowls, Tennis, Golf, Hockey, billiards, and other sports, Cinematograph shows, etc. The permanent directors are: - E. R. Rogers, Central Hotel; J. Williams, 13 Bridge St; D. E. Evans, Gelliwasted Rd; S. C. Hill, Lanwood House, Lan Park; M. Evans, Sportsmans Hotel; W. S. Rasbridge, Queen Adelaide Hotel, Treforest; R. Banfield, Heath House; W. Tucker, High St; Qualification £250. Secretary, G. B. Williams, Registered office, Old Bank Chambers, Market Square, Pontypridd.

On Thurs, Fri, and Sat July 22nd, 23rd and 24th 1920 a Sports and Carnival and Festival was held under the auspices of the Dragons football club. The chief events on Thursday were the Bomb Throwing Competition, Dancing on the Green Competition, and the heats of the 120 Yards Open Handicap. The programme for Friday include the 80 Yards Boys Handicap Race, 130 Yards Whippet Race; Semi-final and final of the 120 Yards Handicap and a 50 Yards Girls Race Under 16 years of age. Saturdays events including a Baby Show Contest for all ages and a cup for Best Baby in Show. There were also seven events for Fancy Dress Costumes, a Male Voice Choir (Minimum of 30 voices) and a Children's Choir Competition. In addition to these there were skipping competitions and competitions for Best Troupe of Boy Scouts, the Best Head of Hair (girls) and Best Head of Hair (women). Each evening there was dancing on the green until 10 p.m.

Welsh Powderhall 1920

The spectators this year totalled a larger number than had been seen at the Taff Vale Park for the Welsh Powderhall than for a long time past. Organisers of other meetings were told that they ought to take a few hints for the orderliness and dispatch in which the programme was conducted. On Monday, when the principal events were, of course, the final of the Powderhall, all roads led to the park, and outside the entrance was gathered a motley collection of vehicles - cars of all ages, sizes and makes, were gathered wheel to wheel with the humbler tradesmen's carts and smart dog-carts. A good humoured sporting crowd of all classes clicked past the bustling turnstiles on to the rapidly filling ground long before the commencements of the sports. Not only from Pontypridd, came these enthusiasts, but from almost every place, large or small, in the principality where the name of sport is known. The winner of the Welsh Powderhall was J. H. Thomas, Pembroke Dock, handicapped at 14 Yards, and he won a brilliant race by about a foot. £100 and a gold medal was the reward for winning the big event. Thomas had taken part in the Welsh Sprint two or three times. He was very popular, and regarded as a good all-round sport, and was described by Mr. Ted Lewis, the starter, as "a very honest competitor"; and he was pleased to see him win. Thomas was 28 years old and turned the scales at 10st.-4 lbs, and had been trained by Mr. Maurice Williams, Pontypridd, and his manager was Mr. Frank Bradley, Pontypridd. However, although beaten for first place, was by no means disgraced, W. Pitman, 17½ Yards, Treforest, securing second place, and J. E. Connelly, 20 Yards, Pontypridd, running a close third, with B. Holloway, 14½ Yards, Bargoed, fourth. The betting on the final beforehand was: Holloway 4-6 favourite, with Thomas and Pitman 6-4 against, and Connelly the 10-1 outsider.

Among the other events, two of the riders in the ¾ Mile Galloway Handicap had exciting and narrow escapes. The first happened whilst rounding the bend near the entrance during the second lap. There was a keen struggle here for the "rails" and the whole field swept round the curve in a state far too contested for safety, when the second horse, which was making valiant attempts to "head" the leader, slipped and fell, throwing its rider, who by a great stroke of luck, rolled clear in the nick of time as the others thundered past. He escaped with nothing more than a rather severe shaking. Just past the near bend, another rider lost his saddle and was dragged for a distance of about ten yards. Happily no serious accident occurred. A notable feature of the galloway and trotting races was the fine riding and keen enthusiasm displayed by the extremely juvenile riders. One would rather imagine these diminutive youngsters in school rather than taking a prominent part in such events, yet there can be nothing but praise for the superb qualities of horsemanship displayed by them.

Walking Race - New Press Box

There was a 12 Mile Walking Race between Jack Isles (Treharris) and Mike Getrych, Pontllanfraith, at the Park for £50, on October 9th 1920, the former winning by a yard. On October 23rd the Pontypridd Observer reported a neatly arranged press box had been fitted at Taff Vale Park by Mr. D. Evans, acting on instructions from the directors of the Dragons club. The box was situated in the grandstand, and a telephone would be installed as soon as the postal authorities could arrange matters. This would enable half-time scores of the English league matches to come direct to the ground. The directors were to be complemented upon their keenness to bring their ground up-to-date.

There was an unfortunate incident in the Dragons home match against Newport County on October 23rd 1920 before some 5,000 spectators. Just before half-time, Owens the Dragons centre-forward, rushed Toone, the visiting goalkeeper, and Toone stopped and punched Owens, whereupon a spectator rushed onto the field and struck Toone. After the interval Toone went up to Owens and apologised and they shook hands, an action which the spectators applauded.

Review

The post-war years had been difficult for Taff Vale Park, the Dragons soccer team seemed to be regaining some of their former glory, and had eventually purchased the park, but the athletics events, and even the Welsh Powderhall had seen a decline in the number of competitors and spectators. The summer's at Taff Vale Park needed a fresh introduction of activities, and the introduction of Carnivals and Civic events would now become very important. However, a big threat to Taff Vale Park came from the grounds at Ynysangharad. Since the turn of the century the fields had been more or less public domain, and more and more events were being held there. There was talk that the Pontypridd Urban District Council were discussing ways of raising money to buy the grounds, and if this became so it would have a material effect on the Taff Vale Park.

Chapter Six 1921-26

Dragons Bid Fails

The Pontypridd Observer of February 12th 1921 reported that the Pontypridd Football association team, the Dragons, had applied to become members of the third division English league for the season 1921-22. A body of local men had purchased the freehold of Taff Vale Park in order that it could be maintained for all time as a football ground. This having been done at a cost of over £4,000. The ground was excellent as far as surface and drainage was concerned, and at this time would accommodate about 15,000 to 18,000, and could be improved to hold 40,000.

Important Soccer Matches

On Saturday April 16th 1921, the Dragons played in the Welsh Cup Final at Ninian Park, Cardiff, where they drew 1-1 with Wrexham before over 10,000 people. The Dragons scored first and their supporters were confident of victory, but an equaliser forced a draw in a game they deserved to win. However, the Dragons lost the replay at Shrewsbury 3-1 before 8,000 spectators. Wrexham scored two goals in the first eight minutes and Ponty never recovered. An injury to one player meant playing the last two-thirds of the match with ten men, and then ten minutes before halftime saw them reduced to nine men, as another player went off injured. On Thursday, April 22nd 1921, the South Wales Senior Cup Final was played at Taff Vale Park, when Bridgend and Ton Pentre drew 2-2.

August Bank Holiday 1921

On Monday, August 1st 1921 a Sports and Whippet Racing Meeting was held in the presence of a large bank Holiday crowd. The events were: 80 Yards Boys, won by J. Garland, Ynysybwl; 100 Yards Open Handicap, won by H. Evelynitrch, Treharris; 300 Yards Open Handicap, won by W. A. Townsend, Llanbradach, and 150 Yard Open Whippet Race won by "Freda".

On August 13th 1921 it was announced that the directors of the Dragons club had during the close season carried out many notable improvements on the ground. Those who would pay their first visit of the season to Taff Vale Park on September 3rd would be surprised at the splendid arrangements made for seeing the game. All that was now needed was the whole-hearted support of the people of Pontypridd and district to build it up and get a name for the town. It would be certainly far cheaper for followers of the winter game to watch a thrilling match at Taff Vale Park than paying train fare to Cardiff and thereby supporting a foreign team. The Pontypridd Observer of August 20th 1921, reported: -

'The Taff Vale Park has changed appearance to that which their supporters were accustomed to last season. One of the great disadvantages was the slippery sloping nature of the bank on the grandstand side. This defect has been remedied effectively. It has been remodelled and steps have been placed right along so that the supporter will not be in any danger of falling over the supporter in front of him. Last season the means of entrance to the ground were far from being sufficient but these have now been increased and renovated in such a manner that a crowd of 25,000 can easily be dealt with. Considerable improvements have also been effected in the dressing room portion of the ground. The old referee's room has been adapted to an office, and the dressing room for the visitors will now contain the referee's room, including bath, etc. The dressing rooms have been enlarged and large baths are now provided for both the homesters and visitors. The grass has been cut and the field looks in the best of condition. The danger of "river ball" is as strong as ever and it has not yet been decided whether there will be an extra charge for the grandstand. The press accommodation has also been improved much to the satisfaction of the pressmen. Mr. O'Rourke, the Dragons team manager, has the full support of the directorate in making any improvements that he considers necessary and much enthusiasm prevails in the camp.'

Welsh Powderhall 1921

A feature of the 1921 Welsh Powderhall on Saturday August 20th and Monday 22nd, was the remarkable manner in which many of the favourites failed to justify the expectations of their supporters. One of the most notable disappointments in the heats on Saturday was the failure of W. R. Applegarth, of London, who, though starting from scratch, was regarded by many as a probable winner. He was beaten with comparative ease in the fourth of twenty heats, and therefore dropped out of the contest. Another failure that day included the previous years winner, J. H. Thomas, Pembroke, and his brother, E. S. Thomas. Several others who were regarded as well in the running, failed to win their heats, with the result that the final stages were made highly interesting, a big element of uncertainty being introduced. After the four semi-final heats, the final, witnessed by a large crowd, was won by G. Williams, Cardiff. He was a strong favourite after the semi-finals, the betting being 5 to 1 on. D. J. Lewis, Aberavon, who came second, was also a fairly warm favourite with many, and only finished a foot behind the winner. The final result was 1st Eddie Williams, Cardiff, 14½ Yds; 2nd, D. J. Lewis, Aberavon, 15½ Yds; 3rd, A. P. James, Dinas, 16 Yds; 4th W. A. Townsend, Llanbradach, 19 Yds. Other events on Monday included a Quarter Mile Galloway Handicap, 1st prize £50; a Quarter Mile boys Handicap, 1st prize £5, won by C. John, Treforest, off 55 Yds; and a 300 Yards Boys Handicap, 1st prize £30, which after eight heats was won by Watcyn Phillips, Mountain Ash.

Wales v Australia (Rugby League) - At Taff Vale Park

In 1921 the Northern Union were still trying to promote the game in South Wales, and approached the leaseholders to stage representative games at Taff Vale Park, and on December 10th 1921, the Welsh Northern Union team were defeated by Australia 16 21, before a gate of 13,000, taking receipts of £991-18s-3d, though the promoters had anticipated a much bigger crowd. The Pontypridd Observer of December 3rd 1921 carried this pre-match report: -

' The occasion will be unique in the history of rugby in Pontypridd. This, I believe, is the first occasion on which this class of football has been played on the park, but it is certainly the first time an international football game has ever been played locally. That there will be a record crowd present goes without saying; some people are

of the opinion that the number will be somewhere in the region of 30 to 35 thousand. The captain of the Welsh side will be W. Gwyn Thomas, the first schoolboy international fullback. "Billy", as he is well know locally, is a Pontypridd boy., and has a host of admirers in the town and district, who will be delighted to see him don his nation's colours on such an auspicious occasion.'

Amongst The Fans

The Rhondda Leader of December 15th 1921 carried this colourful report by "C.L.D." which gives a fascinating account of a big match at Taff Vale Park in the early 1920s: -

"I was amongst the fans, and when I looked up I saw eager eyes, and white, expectant faces of men perched, row upon row, above men. In front were a few lines of wooden benches, and the hard white border that marked the touch-line. I was seated just in front of a little red flag that marked the half-way line, and if I looked to right or left, saw the tall, slender white spaces of the goal posts at each end of the field. Along the edge of the line stolid policemen patrolled with a heavy pad, pad, as their feet met the sodden turf, while over the fringe of grass behind the goal posts to my right, a mounted policeman passed to and fro, his horse clicking and showing the silvery polish of the iron shoes as he lifted his feet cleanly from the ground. Then in the middle of the field stood the Treforest Silver Band, grouped in a ragged curve and trying to appear unaffected by the light, drizzling rain which beat upon their necks and gathered in large, dull lobes upon their instruments. I think the band were playing "Omaha" just then, and I felt a strong desire to get up and sing or dance a stepdance on the press table. Of course, that was impossible. On my right there sat a determined Yorkshire man, who would obviously not stand any nonsense of that sort, and on my left was an old international player, who might have crushed me with his finger. So I could not sing or dance then. I hope to do so the next pay day. Behind the few bleak trees on the far side of the ground rose a bank of slag, which on its top had a siding filled with black coal trucks. Above them, like the top of a shillelagh , rose a hill whose

bleakness was sharply crossed by a few straight lines of terraced houses.

"Pay and take, Pay and take!" the "Monte Carlo Game!" cried a hawker behind me. Then a blind man, led by a little girl, came up for money for some home or other. An argument then began in the press-box. Nobody knew how many spectators were there to see the game. I am very discreet; I waited until two men guessed, and then I named a figure half-way between; they agreed immediately, we are a nation with a love for compromise. Suddenly there was a pitter-patter amongst the photographers, and the band played "The Men of Harlech"; there was a crack of leather meeting leather, and a new ball went up into the air. Someone in a red shirt ran out to catch it, and soon I saw the Welsh team on the field. There was a cheer, but not more than half of the 12,000 people joined in. I suppose the others were studying their programmes. Just then I saw a flight of birds cross high above the field. They passed and repassed three times. Three tries for a Welshman, I thought, perhaps those birds are a good omen. Later I reflected it was a pity they did not know their business better. The band stopped playing and the Australians came on. Perhaps they are not a musical people. At any rate, the band stopped suddenly, just as the first Australian stepped on to the field.

A man at my side asked me for a match. I had none. The man had a very bad memory for he asked me three times for a match. Moreover, he asked at the critical moments. He asked every man near him for a match, and asked so politely that his victim had to turn round even when at the highest pitch of excitement. The Australasians gave their war-cry. It was a strange, guttural song in some Maori dialect. It is a moot point how much that cry helped them to gain victory.

I saw the captains tossing. The Australasians won, and Oliver kicked off for Wales. At first there was not very fast play, but when the Australasian backs set to work I thought the four winds had been let loose. Blinkhorne and Horder moved like quicksilver. No pressman is supposed to feel excited. It is part of his trade to kill the emotions which rise naturally to the breast of every man, for how can one be a fair and critical observer if one is more passionate than a fish? So I sat there and reflected that it was raining; that any sensible man would have been at home, if not in bed, at least in an armchair and with his feet on the mantelpiece. But it was no good. Whenever Burge broke through, and sped like a flash to the line, or when Blinkhorne shot with arrowlike speed straight for the goal, I forgot everything and yelled or drew in my breath sharply, or gave a long, sad "ooh" of dismay. Gronow, Morgan, and Rogers were twinkling in and out like bright stars, when, on a cold and clear evening, you gaze upwards for a long time.

Between the scores and bouts of clean, swift passing by the Australasian backs, the game was not so brilliant as the Welsh rugby of old days. I am not an old man, and I do not believe that we are "going to the dogs" any faster than our grandfathers went, still, I believe that rugby when Bush, Nicholls, Spiller, Trew, Owen, Jones, and other Olympians played, had a glow and a zest in it than even these swift Australasians could not bring to it. The Northern Union rules, too, do not give a game the breathless vigour I had thought to see. Scrummages are short and brisk, and there is no line-out or continual touch finding it is true, yet the essential energy may still be lacking. Very soon Blinkhorne dashed swiftly away, and it seemed that nothing could stop these big, swift colonial's once they had begun to run. Certainly the Welsh players did not tackle well. Some Welshmen behind and about me began to say things which made the Yorkshire man cock his ears. "Bring him down, the _____!" Just then Howley went smartly past and scored for Wales, so the rest of the howl was smothered. I have since been told that these noisy men are Bristolians and Forest of Dean immigrants. I hope so.

Gronow had often tried to kick goals for Wales, and now he succeeded. Although the scores were nearly even, the Australasians were the better team, and soon Burge, Craig and Howley brought back the speed and thrill to the game. When West jumped clean over an opponent I held my breath in fear. Still there seemed to be a great deal of obstruction - which seems a mean and spiteful way of playing. On one occasion Rogers ran up with fine speed, but was stopped in this way by Blinkhorne. Wales had many penalties for *such tricks. Latta and Burge were now playing strenuously and at half-time the Australasians were winning by 16 points to 7.*

A cinema operator began to take photos of me; why I don't know. Possibly he was not aware of my existence, still, I smiled and took off my hat and looked as important as a mere youth can when packed between two men old enough and grave enough to be deacons of any "Set Fawr". Then I saw those birds return and once more fly in a curious order, high across the field. The rain had now ceased, and as I looked up I saw the birds distinctly move into a shape of a great "A" as they crossed the field. They had their wits about them then. As I peered over the Yorkshireman's shoulder the band stopped and the game began again. Wales now played a stronger game. Perhaps it was because of the lemons, or perhaps the new ball helped them.

Woods and Morgan played well and the pack seemed stronger and swifter than in the first half. There were frequent penalty kicks for Wales, who made up in this way what they failed to score in tries, although they pressed near the line. Hurcombe ran through finely, but was recalled for a forward pass. Again the Welsh pressed closely, and nothing but ill-luck withheld them. Gronow and Rogers played finely. At this time the Welshmen began to tackle in a splendid way and the speedy Australasian's were brought down before they had run many yards. Once more, however, Burge dashed through with fine speed and scored just between the posts. Again the Welsh attacked, and Norman had to touch down to save his side. Mr. Mills, of Oldham, was a very keen and shrewd referee, but as the game was generally clean and open, he had little trouble. Wales continued to press, and for the last ten minutes were almost through the line. In the scrums the Welshmen were far superior, and Sullivan's kicking was the best seen. Just then Rogers flashed neatly over from the blindside of a scrum near the line. Gronow converted very finely. Soon the sharp note of the final whistle blew. The Australasians had won 21-16. I think the scores should have been even. Throughout the second half the Welsh forwards were strong and clever, pinning the game close to the Australasian lines. The Welsh backs were somewhat weak. There were moments of fine play.

Spirit and zest were there in abundance, and the game was kept very open and fast. As I walked out I saw the crowds moving up the Broadway. They walked in wave after wave, and one line, moving forward in a ribbon wave, would be pressed on the crest of another. Broadway was lined with motor cars of all sorts, some of which had come into the town at early morning loaded with men eager to see the game. Outside the gates of Taff Vale Park queues had waited since ten o'clock, and all the morning special trains had been pouring in hundreds of men, several of whom previously had never heard of Pontypridd. So the day ended, Pontypridd relapsed into its usual stolidity. "

Dragons In Dire Straights

The same day as the Wales v Australia Northern Union match in December 1921, the Pontypridd Association Football Club held a meeting, and it was revealed that the club had struck another bad patch and had been forced to run heavily into debt. Two months before they had been £3,000 in debt, but this had been reduced owing to the fact that they had sold a few players. Mr. Sid Lewis expressed surprise that instead of their gates getting larger they were getting smaller, and they had the sorry spectacle of trainloads of people going from Pontypridd to Cardiff on Saturdays and other days instead of their remaining at home to support their own club. A voice: *"Cardiff have got the team, and they keep their team!"* Taff Vale Park was doubtless one of the finest grounds in the country, but until they had the use of it under better conditions they could not expect to make the progress they desired. It was eventually decided to request the directors to increase their share of the capital.

1922

A Dragon's Welsh League match against Barry at Taff Vale Park on January 9th 1922 was abandoned 15 minutes before full-time due to a waterlogged pitch. The same week saw the death of Frank Thomas, owner of the "My Hatter" shop in Taff St, and whose suggestion the club wore a dragon on their shirt, and hence came the "Dragons" nickname. After a rugby match between the Glamorgan Police and the Newport Police in the last week of February 1922,

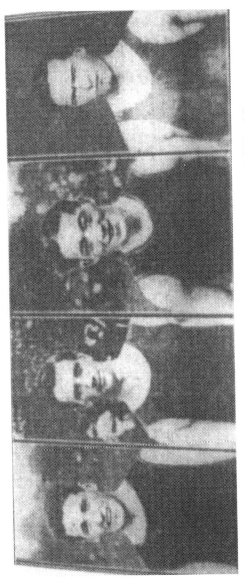

Finalists in 1922 Welsh Powderhall. L to R: Jack Burgess (Cilfynydd), W. Loveluck (Pyle), D. J. Lewis (Mardy), Alun Jenkins (Rhydfelin)

they retired for tea at the Victoria Cafe, where Inspector Rees Davies, an old Pontypridd forward, expressed his regret that the Taff Vale Park could not be secured for the rugby code. In a place like Pontypridd, where rugby had been so prominent in the past, it should have the best ground possible to re-establish it upon its former lines. He volunteered his services for any scheme which may be suggested with the object of acquiring the Taff Vale Park for rugby. A crowd of about 12,000 people watched the Dragons v Porth at the park on April 15th 1922. That summer there was an athletic sports in aid of the Catholic Church Building fund.

Near disaster At Boxing Contest

On Saturday August 22nd 1922 there was a large and enthusiastic crowd at Taff Vale Park where a series of boxing bouts took place. The principal contest was between C. Stone, Taff's Well, and Mog Pugh, Aberavon - 20x3 minute rounds for £50 a side. Pugh was knocked out in the thirteenth round. It was a sensational ending and happened in this way: Pugh wore gum protectors and one of them was knocked off the gum by the blow given by Stone and lodged in Pugh's throat. Medical help was at once forthcoming and luckily the obstacle was removed from Pugh's throat.

Welsh Powderhall 1922

Despite threatening clouds there was no rain to interfere with the heats of the Welsh sprint for the £100 and gold medal and other prizes offered over Saturday, August 19th and Monday 21st in the 1922 Welsh Powderhall. The great sprint was won in fine style on the Monday by W. (Buller) Loveluck, Pyle, who therefore received the £100 and gold medal offered as the first prize. His time constituted a record as far as previous finals of this event were concerned. He got away well from his mark of 16½ yards, and looked like a winner the whole distance. It was a grand race that saw twenty first round heats and four semi-final heats. About halfway Loveluck got up with Jenkins, Rhydyfelin, while a strong effort to get the lead was made by Burgess, Cilfynydd. However, in the next 25 yards the Pyle runner got in front and was closely followed by Jenkins and Burgess. When Loveluck got to the tape he was a foot and a half ahead of the Rhydyfelin representative. A foot divided each of the last three competitors. Loveluck was 27 years of age and at the time played right-wing for the Mountain Ash Rugby Club. The final result of the 1922 Welsh Powderhall was: -

1. W. Loveluck, 16½ Yds, Pyle; 2. A. Jenkins, 18 Yds, Rhydyfelin; 3. J. Burgess, 15½ Yds, Cilfynydd; 4. D. J. Lewis, 12 Yds, Mardy.

In the 300 Yards Open Handicap, after 10 heats, the final was won by G. Rees, Rhydyfelin off 34 Yds. The 880 Yards Open Handicap was won by C. M. Brown, Barry, 40 Yds, who collected £30 and a gold medal. The One-Mile Open Galloway Handicap for £40 was won by "Farmers Boy" owned by Mr. Jenkins, Pencoed. The Six Furlong Open Galloway Handicap for £15 was won by "Little Joe" owned by Mr. Jones, Llanharan.

Seldom, if ever, in the history of the big sprint had the weather been so favourable. The crowd was greater than many had had the courage to hope for even in the absence of rain. The big gate was a clear sign that the meeting was still growing in popularity, and the promoters were again to be congratulated upon the excellence of their arrangements and the splendid success of their efforts. It was pleasing to see the keen interest still taken in the sports by those officials who had been connected with the Powderhall since it started in 1903. Councillor David Williams, for instance was conspicuous by his energy and advice, and Mr. Ted Lewis, the pistol-firer, was as smart and expeditious as ever in the performance of his duties. Then there was Mr. Fred Morris, the timekeeper, whose important task was the stop watch, which he carried out with complete satisfaction. One could mention others, including Mr. Johnny Doran, who has long been associated in a responsible capacity with the sprint which drew some the world's best athletes.

1923

Dragons Purchase Taff Vale Park

By the second week of May 1923, negotiations which had been pending for some time for the transfer of the Taff Vale Park from the former athletic syndicate to the directors of the Dragons association

Taff Vale Park, Pontypridd.

T.V. Park at its best. Circa 1923

club, under the chairmanship of Mr. J. E. Brooks, were finally completed. The directors had felt for some time that the ground should be under their direct control. Hitherto the club had been merely tenants of the ground for the football season only. The new company comprised of the directors of the football club alone. They were to be utilized to foster all forms of sports consistent with football. The Welsh Powderhall and other fixed sport meetings hitherto conducted by the old syndicate would be continued. It was proposed to at once commence extensive alterations on the ground and the erection of a grandstand to accommodate 2,000 people, and the club had put in an early application for inclusion into the third division of the English League. The purchase price of the ground was not disclosed. In July 1923, athletic meetings which included Galloway and Trotting were held, while the work on the construction of the new stand, dressing rooms, and official's quarters at a cost of nearly £4,000 was proceeding. However, there was disappointment when the Dragon's application to join the English League was turned down.

Welsh Powderhall 1923

The 17th annual meeting since the Welsh Powderhall was established 20 years before (the lapsed years being due to the war) did not attract so good a crowd to the Taff Vale Park as had been witnessed at some of the previous events. There were, however, several thousand present to witness some exciting finishes in the foot and horse events. Chief credit for this was no doubt due to councillor David Williams, Greyhound Hotel, who, as in past years, acted as the sole referee and judge, and in no particular instance was his decision called into question. In the One Mile Open Galloway (1st Prize £25) 26 horses entered for the two heats, the final being won by Mr. Lewis's "Queen Rees", Caerphilly. There was also a Six Furlong Open Galloway Handicap with 15 horses, and a 440 Yards Boys Handicap.

For the 130 Yards Welsh Powderhall Sprint, First Prize £100 + Gold Medal, there was a total of 162 entries, and these were divided into 18 heats. Only in one heat did the full compliment leave their marks, the tenth, which was won by T. H. Oldfield, Cardiff, who had won the race in 1911, but he was beaten in the semi-final off 11½ Yds by Howells of Mountain Ash off 13 Yds. Undoubtedly the most popular heat was that of the seventh, which included P. Davies, Broughton Ferry, the well known coloured runner, who was a nominal scratch at 3½ Yds. The manner in which he overtook the other competitors in the last half of the distance won the admiration of the crowd, and he was afforded a rousing reception on leaving the track.

The final had taken place in the presence of an exceptionally large crowd and had ended in a sensational win for Pat Barry, who had never previously gained a success on the track. Off the limit of twenty yards, his start enabled him to beat D. R. Davies in a record time (In 1963 Pat Barry stated that he had run scores of professional races in the previous couple of years deliberately losing so he could obtain a good handicap for this race, and he and his backers won a considerable amount of money on the day as he was a 100-1 outsider before the event!). The race saw the men get off their marks in an exceptionally good start and shot away with great vigour. Barry maintained a lead until near halfway, when Davies commenced to lessen the gap, with Townsend in close attendance. This was continued to the end of the journey, when Barry got to the tape with a yard to spare. The 1923 Powderhall result: 1st Pat Barry, Cardiff, 20 Yds; 2nd D. R. Davies, Abercynon, 16 Yds; 3rd W. A. Townsend, Llanbradach, 16½ Yds; 4th A. W. Howells, Mountain Ash, 13 Yds. The 300 Yards Handicap Final was won by W. A. Townsend. In the Six Furlong Trotting Handicap it was decided not to run the final, and the three heat winners were awarded £5 each.

No Enjoyment at Taff Vale Park

Few spectators, if any, enjoyed the game in comfort at the Taff Vale Park on Monday September 17th 1923, when the Dragons played Ebbw Vale in a Southern League encounter. Rain poured down incessantly from the commencement, and there was no means of getting any shelter whatsoever. Until this is remedied, rainy days would mean a decided reduction in the gates. Many spectators were bemoaning the fact that the old stand had been taken down before a new one was erected. The Dragons won 4-1, but the main thought that was left in the minds of the spectators was, *"when is there going to be any covered accommodation at Taff Vale Park?"* The Pontypridd Observer of October 20th 1923 reported that the new grandstand at Taff Vale Park would be ready soon, and that it really would be an imposing structure and worthy of any ground. It was being erected in an ideal part, and members of the directorate, of the press, and of the sporting public would have an opportunity of witnessing encounters in comfort and from an excellent position. Important improvements had already been carried out and the progressive policy adopted by those closely connected with the organisation was one that could only bring prosperity. In the last week of the same month a sports meeting organised by the Dragons club was held at the ground, and included trotting and Greyhound races.

1924

1924 saw the Dragons football team win the Welsh League, but the summer, apart from the Welsh Powderhall, appears to be bare of the athletic fixtures that had been held the previous years. It is possible that that they were not reported, but it seems likely that the Dragons having bought Taff Vale Park had seen the demise of the Athletic Club, though Teddy Lewis would continue to run the Welsh Powderhall. There were other events held, however, including a carnival in aid of the blind, which was curtailed through bad weather; and the East Glamorgan Agricultural Show. The Dragons successful season, however was marked by some very disturbing occurrences during home games:

On February 18th 1924 Pontypridd played Aberdare in a Welsh Cup match at Taff Vale Park. Two or three incidents happened during the game which infuriated a section of the crowd, and at the final whistle a huge section of the crowd ran riot and made a determined rush for the referee. The official was persuaded by the players to rush to the dressing room, but the players themselves had a rough handling. Duckworthe, the visiting goalkeeper, had a tussle with a collier and had to seek refuge behind the grandstand. Umbrellas were much to the fore and only a timely appeal by Mr. J.E. Brooks saved the situation. The most serious feature was that such scenes would undoubtedly jeopardize whatever prospects the Dragons had of securing admission into the English League division three, and the spectators who fondly imagined themselves as supporters of the Dragons should have realised that such scenes as occurred on this Monday did incalculable harm to the club.

In March 1924 there was a crowd of around 5,000 present for the official opening of the new grandstand at Taff Vale Park that could hold 3,000 persons comfortably. The famous Tottenham Hotspur team were the Dragons' opponents that day, as part of the agreement that saw the transfer of a Dragon player to the London club. However, the crowd was not as big as was hoped, as a heavy fall of snow had fallen overnight. The chairman of directors, Mr. Brooks, in a speech before the game explained that the president of the Southern league was to have done the official opening, but had at the last minute pulled out. Councillor Tom Taylor took his place.

East Glamorgan Show - Aug 2nd 1924

At a luncheon at the Park Schools after this event, Mr. J. E. Brooks suggested that the show should permanently by held at Pontypridd. In the event of such coming to pass he promised them that the Taff Vale Park would always be at their disposal. On August 23rd 1924 the Dragons held its first Annual Horse Show and Carnival.

Welsh Powderhall 1924

During August 9th and Monday August 11th 1924 Pontypridd was the centre of attraction for the whole of the sporting fraternity, not only in the principality, but much further afield. The occasion was the holding of the 18th annual Welsh Powderhall for £140 over a distance of 130 yards, and was the Welsh "Blue Riband" of the track. The official times recorded for the several heats were not as good as in the past. This was not due to any deterioration in the runners, but the change of the running plot from a cinder track to that of grass. For the first time since the inauguration of the great race Councillor David Williams, Greyhound Hotel, was an absentee as sole judge and referee, but his position was filled by his son Ifor. On Saturday the One Mile Open Galloway, 1st prize £25, was won by Mr. Kinsey, Tredegar on "Pussyfoot", the Five Furlong Open Galloway for £15, was won by Mr. Price on "Slack Times;" while the 440 Yards Handicap, for £2-10s, was won by J. Dewar, Cardiff, off 90 yards.

On Saturday there was a total entry of 149 contestants for the Powderhall, and these were divided into 16 heats, being 13 less than the previous year. On Monday, the four semi-finals were won by M. P. Herlihy, Cardiff, off 16 Yds; J. Burgess, Cilfynydd, 14½ Yds; E. G. Williams, Barry, 16 Yds; and Foxwell, Ebbw Vale, 18½ Yds. It was considerably after the scheduled time of 7.30 that the finalists were ordered to "get set". The start was an admirable one, and the excitement great. E. J. Foxwell, who had the advantage of 2½ yards over Herlihy, the favourite, did not hold this long. With a remarkable start Herlihy shot away and outdistanced Foxwell before a quarter of the journey was covered. The Ebbw Valian, however, stuck to the leader with great tenacity, and appeared a dangerous man, but Herlihy maintained his lead. In the meantime Burgess, who had to make up a distance of 1¼ yards from the favourite, let in daylight between him and the Barry representative, and made a grand fight with Foxwell. Herlihy won by a yard, with six inches dividing second and third, and about two yards between third and fourth. Result: 1 . M. P. Herlihy, Cardiff, 16 Yds; 2. E. J. Foxwell, Ebbw Vale, 18½ Yds; 3rd. J. Burgess, Cilfynydd, 14 Yds; 4. E. G. Williams, Barry 16 Yds.

The One Mile Open Trotting Handicap for £40 was won by Mr. Preston's "Miss Freda" off 90 yards; the 880 Yards Open Handicap, was won by J. H. Jones, Tenby; the 300 Yards Open Handicap, was won by R. C. Richards, Ynysybwl, while the Six Furlongs Open Trotting (£15) was won by Mr. Williams' "Towle", from Aberdare.

1925

Boxing returns to Taff Vale Park

On April 3rd 1925 Boxing took place at Taff Vale Park when the main bout was between Danny Morgan, Tirphil, who challenged Billy Moore, Penygraig, to the right of the Welsh Light-weight Championship, but failed to accomplish his desires. The contest, which was for a side-stake of £25 and a promoter's purse, went the whole distance of 20x3 minute rounds before a record attendance. Both men weighed in at the "Horse and Groom" earlier in the day, and both registered a pound under the stipulated weight. When they entered the ring betting was even. Mr. Ted Lewis was stakeholder and timekeeper. The referee's decision in favour of Moore was well received. In another fight Bill Morgan, Tirphil, received a verdict over Tommy Walsh, Porthcawl in 6x3 minute rounds, while a 10x3 minute round fight between Gordon Cook, Penygraig and Willie Vaughan, Clydach Vale, proved a rare slam, which went the whole distance and ended in a draw.

The boxing events seem to take place at regular intervals throughout the Summer of 1925. A sensational incident took place at the end of the eighth round of the principal event of the open-air boxing contest on the T.V. Park on Monday, June 1st 1925. The contest was a 20x3 minute bout for the Bantamweight title of South Wales. The contestants were Sammy Jones, Ystrad, the holder, who was challenged by Johnny Edmunds, Treharris. The earlier rounds were evenly matched, but in the fourth round Jones showed signs of weakness, and about half-way through the eighth round Jones got a nasty jab and went to the boards and nine was counted. At this point the Ystrad man got to his feet, but it was obvious he was in much pain. He was forced to the ropes by the Treharris representative and there received much pummelling. As he was about to go down again, the referee stopped the contest and disqualified Edmunds. Interviewed after the contest the referee said he disqualified Edmunds because he struck Jones while the latter had one knee on the ground. After a count of nine Jones was knocked down again, and it was while he rested on one knee that Edmunds re-commenced to punish him. The decision of the referee came as a surprise to the supporters of Edmunds, who regarded their representative as having fought a clean game.

Welsh Trotting Derby

There was a large crowd present at the races at T.V. Park on Saturday and Monday, June 26th and 28th 1925. The chief attraction was the £100 Welsh Trotting Derby, 1st prize £75, 2nd £5, and 3rd £2. After 3 heats the finalists were Mr. Watts' "Gladys W", 20 Yds; Miss Mintys' "Moss Side", 135 Yds; "Byword", Mr. Johns, Manchester, 85 Yds; and Mr. Bowens' "Direct Chimes", Port Talbot, 105 Yds. "Gladys W" led for the first lap, but before the close of the second "Moss Side" took the lead, followed by "Byword" and "Direct Chimes." The last named went neck and neck for half a lap, with "Chimes" on the outside. Eventually the Port Talbot representative cut in and went well in front and won by nearly four lengths. There was an exciting finish between the other three, "Byword" got 2nd place, with "Marjorie", 3rd and "Moss side" 4th, with "Gladys W" bringing up the rear 10 lengths away.

Mild Sensation at Boxing Event - Dragons Directors Resign

Another large crowd at the T.V. Park for boxing in June 1925 saw in the main event Jack Jones, Merthyr Vale, defeat Charlie Stone, Taffs Well, over 15x3 minute rounds. A scheduled 10x3 minute bout between Joe Leonard, Cwmpark and Billy Wagstaffe, Abercynon, provided a mild sensation. Leonard, an improving young Light-weight, laid the foundations of a points victory in the first four rounds by persistent attacking and crisp hitting, and mid-way through round three he put his man down for a count of eight. He was boxing confidently in the fourth round, when he rushed in to an attack and for a fraction of a second left his chin unguarded. Wagstaffe, the more experienced of the pair, seized his opportunity and sent a right hand to the point. It was perfectly timed and Leonard was counted out.

A meeting of the Dragons Football Club was held at T.V. Park on July 7th 1925, to discuss the future of the club. The old directors had lost a great deal of money last season and were no longer prepared to carry on, with the result that as a company they had disbanded. It was planned to set up a shilling fund to raise money to continue playing. After several meeting it was decided to fulfil the fixtures for the following season, and there were 2,000 spectators present for a trial match at T.V. Park on Monday, August 24th 1925.

On July 25th 1925, for the second consecutive year the East Glamorgan Agricultural Society held their annual show at T.V. Park. There were 700 entries. Special arrangements were made with the railway company to run a special stock train to Carmarthen that evening so that the stock entered for T.V. Park could reach the Welsh National Show at Carmarthen in ample time. At a luncheon at the Park Schools afterwards, Colonel Morgan Linsay, the society chairman, explained that the rules of the society provided that the annual show should be held at Caerphilly, Nelson, Aberaman, Bargoed, Ystrad Mynach, Pontypridd and Llantwit Fardre, many of these places being far more agricultural than Pontypridd, and that the show would not be returning to the T.V. Park next year.

Welsh Powderhall 1925

Dismal weather prevailed on the Monday of the 1925 Welsh Powderhall. The preliminary heats and some other events having been run off on Saturday. A short period before the appointed time for the semi-finals a heavy thunderstorm broke over the district, which most seriously handicapped the attendance. Where as 15,000 or 20,000 usually attended the final, there was not half that number present. In the first semi-final heat S. Smith, Pontypridd, led for a good part of the distance, but towards the tape Pat Barry, Cardiff, 12½ Yds, ran splendidly to the front and won easily. In the second heat E. Morgan, Llanhilleth, 14½ Yds, led from start to finish. The third heat was a keen contest between J. C. Briggs, Tredegar, and Mills, Cardiff, 15 Yds, the latter securing the judges verdict. The fourth heat saw one of the favourites, J. Burgess, Cilfynydd, beaten by only inches after he and Edwards, Abergwynfi, 14½ Yds, kept together, and it was absolutely at the last moment that the latter just got ahead. The final was worth seeing. Morgan sprinted well ahead when less than half the distance had been reached and maintained the lead. He was, however, always closely followed by Barry and Mills, between whom there was a keen race for second place. Half a yard only separated them, while the fourth runner was but a few inches behind. Eddie Morgan received the honour of winning the race and the first prize of £100 and a gold medal. Result: 1st Eddie Morgan; 2nd Pat Barry; 3rd Mills; 4th Edwards.

In the other events J. Burgess, Cilfynydd, made up for losing in the semi-final of the Powderhall by winning the 300 Yards Handicap. There was also an 80 Yards Boys Handicap; a 150 Yards Whippet Handicap; One Mile Galloway Handicap; 440 Yards Boys Handicap; Six Furlong Open Galloway; One Mile Open Handicap and Six Furlong Trotting Dash.

Desperate Dragons Sell Top Players

By the end of October 1925 there were persistent rumours to the effect that the Pontypridd soccer club had finished. The rumour had its origins no doubt from the fact that, owing to the financial state of the club and poor support accorded the committee by the townspeople and followers of soccer football generally, it became imperative to dispense with the services of several of the professionals. However, the committee intended carrying out their obligation so far as this season's fixtures were concerned, and were now engaged in building up a new and considerably less costly team. It had been generally known that Pontypridd, in common with other clubs in the colliery districts, had been hard hit by the depression in the coal trade, but, to their credit, they were one of the few clubs able to meet their financial obligations last season. Being unable to meet the "summer wage", however, they had to dispense with the services of the team which had done so well. In the hope of securing greater support, to meet the prevailing distress in the locality, the committee had decided to reduce the admission to the Taff Vale Ground to 6d, Enclosure 1s, and stand 1s-6d.

The legendary Teddy Lewis

1926

Professional Rugby - Wales v England

A new assault on amateur rugby in South Wales by the Northern Union started with the English profession team defeating Wales 22-30 in a fabulous match on the much improved Taff Vale Park on April 12th 1926, which was now capable of holding up to 40,000 and had a fine playing surface, when a staggering crowd of around 3,000 witnessed the game, the 3,000 seats having been sold out before the game. The receipts totalled £2,301-19s-0d, and 500 to 600 motor cars and innumerable special trains brought spectators into the town, and as far as one could tell there were no accidents. Special police officers were stationed at every corner to direct the traffic and there was a constant stream of carts, charabacs etc. The only fly in the ointment was the fact that the Pontypridd tramcars could not run back and fore every few minutes owing to the great congestion. They did not know whose fault this was, but the enormous benefit the concern would have received in fares was largely lost.

The rugby served up both pleased and disappointed. It pleased in that passing was the general method in piercing the defence, and it disappointed because, after the first ten minutes the trend of play became so obvious. Care-free passing with the occasional reverse pass pleased at first, but presently spectators found themselves anticipating the moves. Wales lost, but they were unlucky in losing J. Jones just before half-time and in having D. Rees limping practically from the kick-off. Their forwards were up against a heavier lot, but they strove manfully against the odds and did astonishingly well with their five forwards in the second half, when they had their backs against the wall. D. Rees was simply handicapped through injury, and at the climax of the game Thompson was carried off. Sullivan missed some easy goal kicks for Wales, but proved very safe when clearing work was necessary.

Things went well for Wales in the first half, when Rosser scored after a nice burst by D. Rees. Jim Sullivan hit the crossbar in attempting to convert, and then Carr equalised for England following some scrappy play. Gallagher then put England ahead with a try from a passing round, and Burgess converted after hitting the cross-bar. Wales fought desperately in the second half, but a burst by Benthon enabled Taylor to get over. Bacon intercepted for Wales to score, and Sullivan converted. Parkin gave the "dummy" for Rix to score another try for England, and Gallagher made the next for Taylor, Burgess converting. Wales came with a rally, E. Morgan and Sullivan getting tries, the fullback converting the first. Splendid passing by England followed and Burgess scored an unconverted try. Rees got another try for Wales, and Benthan followed suit for the visitors. Things were made safe for England when Carr got over with a try which Burgess converted, for though Fowler snatched up the ball and dashed over with an unconverted try for Wales, the odds were too great.

Wales: J. Sullivan (Wigan); F. Evans (Swinton), M. A. Rosser (Leeds), J. Jones, Leeds, J. A. Bacon (Leeds); I. J. Fowler (Batley), Billo Rees (Huddersfield); W. Hodder (Wigan), G. Morgan (Hull), R. C. Roffey (St Helens), J. F. Thompson (Leeds), D. Rees (Halifax), Bryn Phillips (Huddersfield).

This game heralded the formation of a professional rugger team in Pontypridd, who in may 1926 were accepted into the Northern Union code and would compete in the Lancashire section for the 1926-27 season, and in all probability play at Taff Vale Park.

Boxing At The Park

Gordon Cook, Trealaw, beat Tommy Price, Tredegar, at a Taff Vale Park Boxing contest on Saturday May 1st 1926, the referee stopping the bout in the 7th round. Price fought very pluckily, but it was obvious almost from the start that he had little chance against his opponent, who proved to be a more scientific exponent of the art and inflicted heavy punishment. A small angry crowd collected around the referee at the close, and he was bombarded with questions as to his reason for bringing the contest to such an early termination. The police intervened and the disturbers dispersed. Other bouts were fought throughout the afternoon.

PONTYPRIDD ATHLETIC CLUB

The above club have acquired a long lease on Taff Vale Park, have spent nearly £1000 in increasing the accommodation and providing for the comfort of both competitors and spectators and have pleasure in announcing this year's:

WELSH POWDERHALL
TAFF VALE PARK PONTYPRIDD

Saturday, Sept 4th and Monday Sept 6th 1909

SATURDAY - 130 YDS HANDICAP
£144 IN PRIZES
880 YDS - - £30. 1 MILE CYCLE

MONDAY - FINALS
Also 300 Yards Foot Handicap
Half Mile Cycle Handicap

Saturday - Gates Open 3.30} First Event 4.50
Monday - Gates Open 3.30} First Event 5.00

Where Will The Dragons Go?

The professional rugby league side would signal the end for the Pontypridd Dragons association team, who, had finished bottom but one of the Welsh section of the Southern League, and now would have nowhere to play. The Glamorgan County Times of June 5th 1926, carried the following story: -

Unless a suitable ground is secured - and at the present there seems little hope of it, the Dragons Association Football Club (Pontypridd) will not be in existence next season. A local press representative has been authoritatively informed that the ground at Taff Vale Park, Pontypridd, which the Dragons have played on for many years past has definitely been let to the rugby league. He also understands that a grand professional rugby team for Pontypridd has already been practically formed, and that the members of it will compete in the Lancashire section of the league. Soccer enthusiasts in the Pontypridd district are much disappointed at the position of things so far as they are concerned, for they have had the Dragons with them since 1911, and they have rejoiced to know that the old club kept going, even under adverse circumstances and despite the poor attendance's during the last season or two, and the fact that the last team to do service in the Welsh and Southern leagues was purely one of young amateurs. That summer, the Dragons soccer team gave up the fight and disbanded. The directors sold their shares in Taff Vale Park to J. E. Brooks for an undisclosed sum.

Other Sports

On June 19th and 21st 1926, there was Horse Trotting, Foot Racing, and Whippet Racing at Taff Vale Park, and on other occasions throughout that summer. A Walking Match, Sports and Carnival was held on Saturday, June 26th 1926, in aid of the distress fund, and attracted huge crowds, and nearly £30 was realised as a result of the function. Hundreds of people lined the streets to witness the carnival procession and walking match, while there was another excellent attendance at the T.V. Park to witness the sports and termination of the walking races. The sports and carnival were organised by the Entertainment Committee of the Central Distress Committee and the walking matches by the Pontypridd YMCA. Meanwhile, that years Welsh Powderhall athletics meeting at Taff Vale Park ran into problems on August 20th and 22nd of 1926, and the Glamorgan County Times gave this report: -

Welsh Powderhall Sensation

Remarkable scenes were witnessed on the Taff Vale Park on Monday evening in connection with the semi-finals of the Welsh Sprint of 130 yards. Nothing approaching such a demonstration had been witnessed during the previous 19 annual meetings. The trouble arose over the disqualification of A. J. Bevan, New Tredegar, who won his handicap on the Saturday off a 20 yard mark. An objection was lodged against him and Bevan was notified by wire on Sunday that he was to appear before the committee on Monday to produce his age certificate. The allegation was that he had given the wrong information on his entry form and had calculated to mislead the handicapper. His father came to Pontypridd early on Monday morning with the desired information and during the afternoon appeared before the authorities. As a result of this Bevan was disqualified by the handicapper. In the meantime, D. Richards, of Cadoxton, Barry, who was off 16½ yards, had been summoned to substitute for Bevan because he ran second in the heat. So far as the general public were concerned the announcement on the field that Bevan had been disqualified was accepted. However, as the time approached for the running of the semi-finals, the rumour was circulated that the superior officials had over-ridden the findings of the handicapper and that Bevan would run. This incident was confirmed when the man came out for the second heat of the semi-final. Bevan was then on the ground in his racing colours. Immediately he was seen there arose from the crowd a hubbub of cheers and booing. Mr. Danny Davies, on behalf of the book-makers, approached the officials in the enclosure, and the general attitude of the crowd became so menacing that Mr. J. E. Brooks, the secretary of the Taff Vale Syndicate, who were promoters of the sports, stepped into the breach, and pointing to Bevan, the New Tredegar runner and said "This man will run ." This led to another

outburst, and the running of the second heat of the semi-final was
suspended for ten minutes to allow the excitement to abate.

Asked for an explanation of the matter, Mr. Brooks said: - *"An*
objection had been laid by a runner against A. G. Bevan, and this
was considered by the officials on the ground and after hearing all
the evidence it was decided by the handicapper to withhold the
objection." At a subsequent meeting of the directors it was decided
to over-rule the decision and allow Bevan to run. Bevan went on to
win the semi-final and final, the placing's in the final being: - 1. A.
G. Bevan, New Tredegar, 20 Yds; 2. G. Evans, Barry, 14½ Yds; 3.
E. G. Brown, Treforest, 16½ Yds; 4. G. T. Morgan, Machen, 18
Yds. The officials at this meeting were: Judge, Mr. Ivor Williams,
Greyhound Hotel; Timekeeper, Mr. Fred Morris; Starter, Mr. Ted
Lewis; Handicappers: - Foot, Mr. J. Doran; Horse, Mr. J. Price,
Merthyr; Clerk of Scales, Mr. J. Belli; Secretary, Mr. J. E. Brooks,
88 Taff Street.

Pontypridd Rugby League Team Begins

The 1926 General strike and its aftermath - a bitter seven month
miners strike and lock-out had left the South Wales economy in a
state of crisis, with coal and steel production falling, and Pontypridd
itself was in the thick of the fight of both the General Strike and
miners' strike. This was the background to the new Northern Union
Club, Pontypridd, the only one in South Wales between the wars.

Early in August 1926 the Pontypridd rugby league club announced
exceptionally reasonable charges for members tickets in all sections
for the coming season. Members could have a reserve seat in the
stand for 25/-; and the opportunity to retain their seats for the New
Zealand match on Christmas Day. There are also stand tickets
(reserved and under cover) for 21/-; while lady members tickets
were only 13/-. Persons desirous of taking advantage of supporters
club tickets could do so by joining the organisation, which was open
to all persons within a radius of 60 miles of Pontypridd. Sub-
committees of the supporters club could be formed in any town or
district within the above mentioned limit, and supporters club
members would get priority for ground or enclosure tickets for the

New Zealand match. The enclose was capable of holding 6,000 persons, and tickets for the season were only 16/- (less than 1/- per match). The attractive fixture list had already been published and in view of the interesting programme the prices were without doubt the most reasonable in Wales. Applications could be made to the Hon. Sec, Taff Vale Park, or Mr. J. E. Brooks, Tobacconist, 88 Taff Street, or the Hon. Sec. Supporters Club, Taff Vale Park, Pontypridd. A meeting was called to form a supporters club in connection with the Northern Union and was held in the grandstand on the Taff Vale Park on a Monday night. Mr. G. Leake (Newport) the secretary of the Pontypridd club, and one of the three members of the league commission in Wales, invited subscriptions of 10/; and added that if the necessary membership was secured, a portion of the ground would be allocated to the supporters, and there was the prospect of a covered stand being erected on the river end.

The number of people present at the final trial of the Pontypridd Rugby League club at Taff Vale Park on August 28th 1926, and the enthusiasm displayed warranted the feeling that the prospects of the organisation were bright. It was one of the most exhilarating games seen on the ground for a long time. A large portion of the spectators had for several seasons at the park witnessed Association Football, and they were not disappointed (wrote a rugby league correspondent!) when the Dragons went out of existence. But the performance on this occasion filled them with delight, and they were looking forward with pleasure to the important fixtures which had been arranged. There were over 10,000 spectators present for the first home match against Oldham and 6,000 for the second, and although Pontypridd were somewhat heavily defeated, their performances warranted meritorious comment. The results of the Pontypridd Rugby League club, whose colours were White, Red, and Navy Blue (Captained by Jerry Shea) are as follows: -

Pontypridd Rugby Club - Northern Union - Season 1926-27

1926					F A
Aug	28th	Final Trial			
Sept	4th	Oldham	Home Lost		15-23

	11th	Swinton	Home	Lost	5 -28
	18th	Salford	Away	Lost	7 -20
	25th	Leigh	Home	Lost	3 -11
Oct	2nd	St Helens	Away	Lost	13-35
	9th	Widnes	Home	Won	17-15
	16th	Wigan	Away	Lost	15-23
	23rd	Swinton	Away	Lost	3 -20
	30th	Leeds	Away	Lost	7 - 8
Nov	6th	Rochdale Hornets	Home	Won	11-10
	13th	Wigan Highfield	Away	Draw	0 - 0
	20th	"	Home	Won	10- 3
	27th	Barrow	Away	Lost	3 - 8
Dec	4th	Wales v N.Z. - T.V. Park			
	11th	St Helens	Home	Lost	0 - 5
	18th	Broughton Rangers	Away	Lost	5 - 8
	25th	New Zealand	Home	Lost	8 -17
	27th	Leigh	Away	Lost	3 -12
,1927					
Jan	1st	Barrow	Home	Won	9 - 3
	8th	St Helens Rec.	Away	Lost	6 -13
	15th	Warrington	Home	Lost	8 -13
	22nd	Wigan	Home	Lost	5 -13
	29th	Warrington	Home	Won	12- 0
Feb	5th	Widnes	Home	Lost	5 - 6
	12th	Widnes	Away	Lost	2 -23
	17th	Hull	Away	Lost	0 -26
	26th	Hull	Home	Won	18- 8
Mar	5th	Rochdale H.	Away	Lost	0 -16
	12th	Salford	Home	Won	13- 5
	19th	Batley	Away	Lost	7 -16
	26th	St Helens	Home	Lost	5 -10
Apr	9th	Leeds	Away	Lost	6 -27
	16th	Warrington	Away	Lost	8 -21
	18th	Broughton Rangers	Home	Lost	3 -17
	23rd	Batley	Home	Won	10- 8
	25th	Oldham	Away	Lost	3 - 6
	30th	Glamorgan v Mon. T.V. Park (18-14).			

As with many teams in their first season Pontypridd had faced an uphill task. However, the biggest score they conceded was only 35, and 13 of their 24 defeats had been by less than 10 points. But crowds had declined, partly reflecting the economic situation, and partly due to the teams lack of success. They finished 27th out of 29 teams, but the other newcomers, Castleford, finished bottom. However, Castleford would go on to better things. Pontypridd's end of season record was:

P32, W7, D1, L24, For 223 pts, Against 447, Points 15, Perc. 23.43

Professional Rugby - N. Z. At Taff Vale Park Twice

In the winter of 1926 the New Zealand professional rugby team was touring the British Isles, and on December 4th 1926, they were defeated 34-8 by Wales on Taff Vale Park, before 18,000 spectators. Nine public houses had secured an extension of opening hours, from closing at 3.30 until 6 p.m. The match would finish about 4.15. The Stipenduary who had granted permission hoped that there would be facilities for the supply of food, such as sandwiches. On announcement of the fixture the local community took the chance to show its hospitable character. John Leake, the chairman of the Pontypridd R.L.F.C. wrote to the council suggesting the Kiwis should be afforded a civic reception. On their arrival on Friday night one of the choirs that had been competing in the eisteddfod was departing, and in honour of the visitors they sang a chorus. It was much appreciated and delighted the New Zealanders. On Saturday morning there was a reception at the council chamber and the chairman, Mr. John Howell, J.P, delivered a speech that was worthy of the prime minister welcoming his cousins from the other side of the world. On the morning of the match the tourists were given a charabanc tour, and in the course of the trip they visited the Great Western Colliery and the South Wales Power Company's works and were shown the wonderful machinery there by Councillor Roper. One of the local councillors told the visitors that "if you ask Mr. Evan Williams perhaps he will let you down Dan's Pit (Pwllgwaun Colliery), but you will have to go down one at a time!" The tourists response was unrecorded. The Kiwi tourists also placed a wreath at the war memorial on the Common, to commemorate the dead of the

The Rugby Football League

....

Souvenir Programme

NEW ZEALAND
V
WALES

At Taff Vale Park, Pontypridd
DECEMBER 4th, 1926

Kick Off at 2.45 p.m.

....

Price   - -   **Threepence**

This is the only Official Programme and
Souvenir of the Match

Printed by Percy Phillips - Observer offices

First World War. Wales won the game but the New Zealanders were given a warm reception. Before and after the game they were given tea at the Park Hotel, Taff Street, during which Mr. J. E. Brooks, the chairman of the local Rugby League Committee, said they much appreciated the support shown by the council. As they knew he himself had been a sportsman all his life, and that day they had made a huge step forward and the match had been a scientific and spectacular treat. He referred to the splendid sportsmanship shown by both sides and said they could not take exception to any part of the game as being unsportsmanlike. He was happy to see the leading citizens of the town in the persons of the District Councillors endorsing the game and he appreciated their support. He would endeavour to secure for Pontypridd a fare share of the important fixtures and get the best teams for Pontypridd. He thanked the chairman and council for entertaining them. The Welsh team that faced N.Z. was: -

Sullivan, (Wigan); Rhondes, (Pontypridd), Hurcombe (Halifax), Lewis (St.Helens), Evans (Swinton), Caswell (Hull)., Rees (Swinton), Hodder (Wigan) Oliver (Pontypridd), Green (Pontypridd), Stevens (Wigan), Davies (Pontypridd), Gore (Salford). Reserves , Owen and Roffery.

On Christmas Day 1926 the New Zealand team returned to play the Pontypridd team, but did not attract such a very large crowd but won 17-8 before 10,000 spectators. This was the colonials' first match since the healing of differences between their manager and the Rugby League Committee, which in the earlier part of the week threatened the entire suspension of the tour. Their team fielded as selected, but contrary to their general custom they at once lined up for the kick-off without giving their war song. The demands of the crowd, however, were insistent, and the referee held up the opening signal for an abbreviated rendering of the song.

Early on, after some close tackling in mid-field, Davidson broke through, and with a remarkable run got over with New Zealand's first try. Delgrossi added the extra points. Some inter-change of passes amongst the Pontypridd men, going from one touch line to the other, culminated in Loveluck failing to hold the ball from a long throw. Maintaining their pressure, Clant passed the ball, and in a tricky manner, for Green to score behind the visitors' posts. Fairfax missed one of the easiest possible opportunities to add the extra points. From a dribbling movement which Pontypridd could not stop Mason fell on the ball over the goal line, which Delgrossi failed from an awkward angle to improve upon. Two minutes later Davidson passed the ball out to Brown near the halfway line, and an exciting race was witnessed between him and Curtis. Roberts, too, cut across to impede New Zealand's progress, but the latter eluded him and scored the colonials' third try of the match in the extreme corner. Attempts by the home forwards finally met with success when Curtis, taking a pretty pass from a scramble, got over with a try, to which Shea added the points. The visitors, however, added to their lead by tries through Avery, and Davidson, neither of which was improved upon.

Pontypridd: J. Roberts; A. Curtis, J. Shea (c), W. Brown and W. R. Loveluck; P. Oakley + S.V. Fairfax; A. Green, G. Oliver, J. Grant, W. Cox, J. Hellings, D. Thomas.

New Zealand: Kirwin; Desmond, Cole, Davidson and Brown; Delgrasso + Hall; Menzies, Parkes, Herring, Mason, Thomas, Avery (c).

Review

The early 1920s had seen the demise of the Pontypridd Athletic Club and the Dragons. Professional soccer had been replaced by professional rugby. Athletics had now become rare events, even though the Powderhall was still allowed to continue, but even this was suffering from poor crowds, and the competitors were now mainly local rather than international athletes. Cycling had declined to a few minor events. How long would the Pontypridd Rugby League team survive and what could been done by the leaseholders of Taff Vale Park to bring back the crowds?

Chapter Seven 1927 to 1931

Semi-National Eisteddfod A Success

Extensive preparations had been made for the holding of the Pontypridd Semi-National Eisteddfod, which took place at Taff Vale Park on June 30th , July 1st & 2nd 1927, and the promoters of the meeting fully justified their enterprise, for the event was a huge success. There were about 900 entries in all. The Eisteddfod which was organised under the auspices of the Temple Baptist Church, Graig, was excellently stewarded. Events included: - Ladies Choral; Soprano Solo; Contralto Solo; Boys Solo, Under 16; Junior Recitation Under 14; Children's Pianoforte; and many others.

On July 7th 1927 a Pontypridd School Sports Day was held at Taff Vale Park on a Friday afternoon. The proceeds were in aid of the Pontypridd Cottage Hospital, the Blind Institute, the Teachers Benevolent and Orphanage Fund, and the Ynysangharad Park. Great enthusiasm was evinced in various events, while an attractive feature of the programme was the physical drill display by groups of girls and boys under Miss E.Davies.

A Stark Warning

At the Pontypridd R.F.C. A.G.M. at the end of July 1927, the club secretary, Mr. W. Berriman gave this word of warning to young local footballers who might being thinking about playing professional rugby for the Pontypridd team next season:

"They must not think that they can go down to Taff Vale Park and participate in Rugby League and then come back to the Ynysangharad Park and expect to take part in the amateur code. Once they took part in the Northern Union match they were for ever, so far as the Welsh Union was concerned, debarred from playing any more Welsh football encounters in the amateur sense, and the door would be closed forever."

Around the same time the "Times" reported that it was definitely officially announced that the Taff Vale Park which has been leased for Greyhound Racing, would be available for the Pontypridd Rugby

League club and for the county championship matches. On Monday, August 1st 1927, The East Glamorgan Agricultural 32nd Annual Show attracted a fair attendance at Taff Vale Park.

The Glamorgan County Times of August 6th 1927 carried this report

ELECTRIC HARE COURSING - PONTYPRIDD LEADS WAY

Company To Take Over the Taff Vale Park

To Pontypridd will fall the distinction of pioneering the new sport of Electric Hare Coursing in Wales. The site selected for the track being the Taff Vale Park, where the Welsh Powderhall has been run annually, and which last year became the home of Rugby League football in the principality, and has passed through many vicissitudes since the days when it was first laid out by ex-councillor David Williams, Greyhound Hotel, on behalf of the syndicate. It is now owned exclusively by Mr. J. E. Brooks, tobacconist, of Taff Street. In conversation with Mr. Jack Brooks (son of J. E. Brooks) I was informed that about three weeks ago three members of the White City Electric Hare Racing Association visited South Wales. They had in view the acquiring of either the Ely Racecourse, Cardiff, or the Taff Vale Park, Pontypridd. Upon inspection of the latter they are reported to have said that there was it was a "typical White City ground". Terms were submitted for the lease of the ground for three years with an option of a further extension. Large sized photographs of the ground showing the entire track with the stand, offices, etc; and the available space for the construction of kennels were submitted to the board of directors in London.

Mr. Brooks added that it was evident that the Ely racecourse was not available for the object in view, and in a communication received on Monday, the promoters agreed to the terms offered, with some slight modifications. The promotion would commence forthwith, the preparation of the ground which they have taken over from last Saturday. The construction of a large number of kennels would be proceeded with and also the laying down of the electric track on the ground, which was the same dimensions as the White City, London. The present paddocks which has accommodation for "parking" several hundred motor-cars will be converted into kennels, as many of the dogs will be kept there all the year round. In all probability two meetings will be held each week. Asked what would become of the Rugby League football this season, Mr. Jack Brooks replied, "They will have to look for a new ground as far as we are concerned". Last year Mr. J. E. Brooks was one of the directors of the Pontypridd Rugby League Football Club and chairman of the local committee. Subsequently, I had a conversation on the 'phone with Mr. J. L. Leake, Newport, the financial secretary of the Welsh Rugby League Commission, on the matter of the playing ground for the coming season, and he stated that he had been informed of the proposed changes at Taff Vale Park, but that this would not interfere with the matches for the new season. Mr. Eban Jones, who is the newly appointed secretary of the Pontypridd R.L. Club, expressed himself in a similar manner, and added that last week three members of the R.L. Commission visited Pontypridd, and that every arrangement was in progress for the continuation of the club upon the progressive lines adopted last year.

However, at the back of the same issue, a different story was being told: *The Greyhound Racing and Breeding Club of Great Britain Ltd, whose registered offices are 29a Charing Cross Road, London, has the option of the Taff Vale Park greyhound racing at Pontypridd. This company has no connection with the White City Syndicate. The new company is increasing its present capital to £50,000 and will operate the Pontypridd track and other tracks in Cardiff, Brighton and another one in London. The Taff Vale Park will be available for the use of the Pontypridd Rugby League Club up until the end of December. It is expected that the track will be ready for greyhound racing by Easter Monday next.'* The Course Hare Racing, or Greyhound Racing, as it was normally called, would begin in the summer of 1928 and run almost unreported until 1930.

1927 Welsh Powderhall

The 21st annual meeting of the great Welsh Sprint, which for years was known as the Welsh Powderhall, was held at Taff Vale Park on Saturday August 13th and Monday 15th 1927. Although prizes of

£140 were offered for the premier race of 100 yards, which in days gone by would have attracted some of the best sprinters, either the bigger money of modern day forms of sport or the industrial depression was responsible in a great measure for the depleted attendance, and there could not be more than a couple of thousand present. The climatic conditions in the morning, too, were a big factor in the attendance. The Powderhall race was very keen, and the other competitions were of a good standard. The winners of the semi-finals on Monday were: L. Stevens, Cardiff; L. Jenkins, Abercynon; Les Thomas, Treforest, and George Cowdell, Tredegar. In the final the men got away well from their respective marks to a very good start. The subsequent race was one of the best and most evenly contested finishes that had been witnessed on the T.V. Park for several years. Although there were not the prominent and high-class runners that had adorned the track, the contest revealed some close handicapping work by Mr. Johnny Doran. George Cowdell, who ran well in the semi-final, justified his position and maintained his place as favourite. He was a leading marksman of the finalists and maintained his position until a third of the distance had been covered, when Stevens began to reduce the space between himself and Cowdell. In the meantime Jenkins, who was the back marker of the bunch, got into his stride, and picking up well from his mark, shot in front of Thomas when 20 yards from the tape. Thus, the four men reached the tape almost in a bunch, and only inches divided the first three, their official places being: 1st, J. Cowdell, 16½ Yds; 2nd, L. Stevens, 15½ Yds; 3rd, L. Thomas, 14 Yds; 4th, L. Jenkins, 12½ Yds. The winner was a comparatively young man, and although he had entered for previous Powderhalls at Pontypridd, he had never competed, and was a miner at the Tytrist Colliery, Tredegar.

The Pontypridd Rugby League Team disband

In August 1927 the Pontypridd Rugby League team started their second season. Of the 25 players signed for the clubs second season, only four had experience of Northern based Rugby League clubs, and despite showing promise the club struggled. There was concern before the season started that the ground had been leased to a greyhound racing syndicate, but it was later confirmed that it would

Official   Programme

The Rugby   League

PONTYPRIDD
RUGBY FOOTBALL CLUB

v.

Rochdale Hornets

Taff Vale Park, Pontypridd.

Saturday, September 17th, 1927.

PRICE 2D.   SEASON 1927-28

Pontypridd Rugby Football Club.

COMMITTEE.

Chairman—Mr. ARTHUR BROWN   Treasurer—Mr. W O THOMPSON
Hon Sec—Mr A A JONES   Hon Treas—Mr JOHN L LEAKE
Messrs A PARNALL, J BROOKS, J WILLI, A BEXTON, D CAMPBELL
H MITCHELL, A WARLOW, D ROGERS, A KITE

Our Play and Our Players.

I quite well have taken particular notice of teams at matches the Rochdale team who played here last Saturday and so forth of our last home match, and may say that our last home match so forth ...

[remaining text illegible]

be available for Rugby League. After six straight defeats the Pontypridd clubs first win came against Barrow on October 8th at Taff Vale Park before a crowd of less than 1,000 and thoroughly deserved the 13-7 victory. On October 15th 1927 the Glamorgan and Monmouthshire Rugby League team defeated Cumberland at Taff Vale Park. However, the Pontypridd teams future was suddenly cast into doubt. Only a week later, the club would play its final game which, like the first at Taff Vale Park, was against Oldham. The receipts were only £24. So what brought about its end? Reports that greyhound racing had leased Taff Vale Park were true, but the team had a contract to use the ground until the end of 1927 However, the main reason seems to have been the trade depression, i.e. unemployment, which accounted for disappointing takings which made it impossible to balance receipts and expenditure at Taff Vale Park. The final accounts showed a loss of £1,393 including £730 owing to the Rugby League Council, with assets of only £75. However, a local amateur Northern Union League Competition started at the end of November 1927 with sides including Rhydyfelin, Nantgarw, Pantygraigwen, Cilfynydd Rangers, and Taff Vale Athletic. Another era at Taff Vale Park had come to an end. The result of the professional clubs last season are as follows: -

Pontypridd Rugby Club - Northern Union 1927-78

1927					F	A
Aug	27th	Leigh	Away	Lost	0	-17
Sept	3th	Bradford Northern	Home	Lost	8	-11
	10th	Wigan Highfield	Away	Lost	7	-20
	17th	Rochdale Hornets	Home	Lost	5	-14
	24th	Castleford	Away	Lost	6	-26
Oct	1st	St. Helens Rec.	Away	Lost	0	-40
	8th	Barrow	Home	Won	13	- 7
	22nd	Oldham	Home	Lost	5	-14

Playing record Played 8, Won 1, Drew 0, Lost 7, Points for 48, Points against 149.

1928

Powderhall to Stay at Pontypridd

The Pontypridd Observer of August 18th, 1928, wrote: - *'General satisfaction is expressed in South Wales pedestrian circles with the decision to run the famous Welsh Powderhall handicap at the Taff Vale Park instead of at Pandy Park Caerphilly. At first it was feared the possibility of greyhound racing at Pontypridd would necessitate taking the race from its home, but thanks to influential sportsmen the "old Park" has been retained . The race will take play on August 25th and 27th.'*

New Track - New Sport For Pontypridd

The Pontypridd Observer of May 18th 1929 gave this account of a new layout for the racing track at Taff Vale Park, and the introduction of a new sport: -

Dirt Track Racing - A Thrilling Sport

' One of the most popular, exciting and thrilling sports is Dirt Track Racing. It was introduced from Sydney a few years ago and has become extremely popular. Mr. J. E. Brooks, who is always up to date, decided some time ago to equip the Taff Vale Park as a dirt speedway track and so well has he succeeded that the experts are unanimous in their praise of the new track. The cement track has been removed and replaced by a cinder track six inches deep. Thousands of tons of ashes, sifted six times have been used. The whole is surrounded by match boarding which is far superior to wire netting. The track will be opened on Monday and there will be races every Saturday during the summer and if a success the track will be electronically illuminated and racing continued during the winter. Six loudspeakers will be provided and everyone will be able to hear the announcements. Once more the Taff Vale Park will become the home of sport and Broadway will be crowded with pedestrians, motor cars, charabancs, etc; all making for the dirt track. '

On Monday May 20th 1929 the new track at Taff Vale Park was opened. Mr. J. E. Brooks welcomed all present by means of the loudspeaker and said he hoped they would have an enjoyable evening. The promoters were determined to give of the best sport attractive in every way. Crack riders would take part. Chief interest was centred in the Mile Race of Cardiff v the Valleys, in connection with which there were nine heats, and at the close of which the points registered each were equal at 26. The track record was set up by R. H. Baker, Merthyr.

On Thursday evening June 1st Syd Parsons, Australia, set up a new record for the Taff Vale Park dirt track. The programme opened with the first of three challenge races between Parsons and R. H. Baker, Merthyr. Baker's machine broke down, and Parsons covered the distance in a new record, the previous record having been held by Baker. Parsons won the match by winning the second race. Prior to the commencement of the racing the spectators witnessed Frank Moody giving a boxing exhibition in a ring set up in front of the grand stand. Moody, who was preparing under the care of Mr. Llewellyn Williams for his contest with Pierre Galdwin, France, at Manchester, boxed three rounds each against his brother Glen and Billy Green, Taffs Well. This was the first time that Dirt Track Racing had been staged at the Taff Vale Park in mid-week, but the large attendance justified the experiment. Mr. J. E. Brooks intended to repeat it in the near future.

Porth Runner Wins Cambrian Dash

On Monday, June 10th 1929, a young and hitherto unknown runner in the person of A. Mower, Porth, won the 80 yards Cambrian Dash. Mower, who ran off 12½ yards and covered the distance in 7.8 seconds, is 23 years old and started his career as a sprinter last season. The second was W. Jones, Cilfynydd, who, in addition to being a good performer on the track, was a well known rugby footballer, playing right-wing threequarter for Cilfynydd. Last season he had the distinction of being the champion try getter for Cilfynydd. One of the most exciting finishes in the history of the Cambrian Dash was provided by the final, Mower and Jones being separated by inches only at the tape. C. G. Trengenna, Penygraig and Bryn Davies, Pontypridd, were third and fourth. There was also a

150 yards Whippet Handicap with several heats, resulting in the final being won by "Sult" of Mountain Ash.

Dirt Track Racing And More Entertainments

On June 15th 1929 there was another good attendance for Dirt Track Racing. However, having regard to the bad weather, when the rain commenced to fall heavily, Mr. J. E. Brooks, following his usual practice, invited all the spectators to avail themselves of the shelter of the grandstand whether they had paid grandstand prices or not. In order to encourage young motor cyclists to take up the sport, Mr. Brooks had thrown the track open to them between 5 p.m. and 7 p.m. on Tuesdays, Wednesdays, and Thursdays, and already some promising talent had been uncovered. The Motorcycle Dirt Track Racing was now very strong, and large attendances were common. On July 6th the Pontypridd Observer carried this report that shows that Mr. J. E. Brooks had several ideas about how to attract people to Taff Vale Park: -

'The large attendance at the dirt track racing at Taff Vale Park on Saturday evening last, thoroughly enjoyed the musical programme provided at the intervals by the loud speaker supplied by Mr. D. G. Ball. There is no doubt that this powerful wireless set has been a great source of attraction and we congratulate the promoters upon engaging local enterprise.' Promising new talent was on show that evening and there was a particularly exciting finish in the second of five heats of the Great Western (rolling start) Scratch Race for £5, £3, £2 and £1 respectively. "Hurricane" Hampson and "Whirlwind" Baker, both from Cardiff, came first and second respectively. Only one-fifth of a second separated them, the time being 1 min - 39 secs. Other events included the Glyn Taff Handicap and the Llanover Handicap, both won by Y. Davies, Upham.

On July 13th 1929, Mr. J. E. Brooks, the promoter of dirt track racing at the Taff Vale Park announced to the spectators that some of the biggest "stars" of the D.T.R. world would be seen on the track before long. Among them being "Sprouts" Elder of California, the champion of the world, who had been booked to appear on the Taff Vale Park on August 15th.

**Thomas D Lougher, Pontypridd's 17 year old
speedway prodigy 1927**

Thrills and Spills at Dirt Track Racing

There were thrills and spills on Saturday July 17th 1929 in the Dirt Races. The "Three Challenge Races" between T. D. Lougher, Pontypridd, and C. Phillpots, Newbridge, was a draw after two races, but when the final race came about Lougher discovered that his machine was damaged. Nigh Carter, Brynmawr, came to his rescue, and offered the Pontypridd lad his machine. But Lougher lost the final race by half a lap. However, after five heats of the Garth Handicap Race (Rolling Start), Lougher had his revenge by winning the final. The Brecon Scratch Race and the Sugar Loaf Scratch Race (Rolling Start) were won by George Gregory.

The following Saturday, July 22nd 1929, there was another large crowd to witness the Dirt Track Racing, when attacks on the track record by "Red" Murch, America, and Len Parker, Bristol, failed. There was a sensational finish to the final of the Cambrian Dash Race. Luke, Cardiff, and Key, Bristol, and Phillpots, Newbridge, were racing together, when on going round a bend one of the machines collapsed, and so near were the other three that an accident was unavoidable. Phillpots sustained the greater injury, but this did not prevent him being desirous of going on again. The restart was held up until Dr. McDonald Mitcher had examined the rider and declared him unable to participate. Therefore the other three contested the final and Luke, Key and Parker finished in that order. In the final of the Welsh Powderhall Handicap (What an original name!) the machines of Ivor Luke and Len Parker broke down and Y. Davies, Bridgend, had an easy win.

August 1st 1929 saw interest in the Bristol v "The Valleys" match Dirt Track Racing, but local enthusiasm was brought to its highest pitch by a Triangular Race between three local men, D. T. Morgan, Caerphilly, and D. H. John and T. D. Lougher, Pontypridd, when the last named won the rubber in magnificent time. Lougher also won the Graig-Y-Don Handicap, while Parker, after four heats, won the final of the Brig-Y-Don Scratch Race.

155

TAFF VALE PARK
SPEEDWAY

Saturday, September 14th 1929
Flying Twelve
(All Scratch Riders)

Baker	Luke	Upham	Price
Hampson	Parker	Douglas	Gregor
Carter	Hill	Wade	Clibbett

HANDICAP RACE - SCRATCH RACE

ALSO THE FOLLOWING RIDERS

John	Lougher	Aplin	Watkins
Fowler	Longney	Dunlop	Lyons

NOTE CHANGE IN TIME OF START

Gates Open 3-30   First Race 5-30

Admission - Boys 6d;   Ground 1/2;   Stand 2/ (Including Tax)

Unemployment cards must be shown - 9th week.

Welsh Powderhall 1929

For the first time, on August 7th 1929, in the long history of the Welsh Powderhall, which was established in 1903, the event was won by a Pontypridd lad. The achievement was secured by Bryn Davies in the final at Taff Vale Park on Tuesday, whilst Len Thomas, Treforest, ran a close second. The attendance on both days was disappointing, and had a strange contrast to the years gone by when the event attracted a crowd of many thousands. There were 99 entries, and these were divided into sixteen heats, but in no particular instance did the full compliment face the starter. In one of these heats there was a walk-over.

In the final the four men got away to a brilliant start. At forty yards Bryn Davies overtook Dawe and thus got into the lead. Although Cowdell made heroic efforts to gain his second Powderhall, he was unable to do so, but ten yards from the line he passed Dawe, after which there was a dour struggle, but both the Pontypridd men kept the lead, and Bryn Davies won by a yard whilst inches divided Len Thomas and Cowdell, Dawe bringing up the rear two yards behind. Final Result: 1st. Bryn Davies, 15½ Yds, Pontypridd; 2nd, Les Thomas, 14½ Yds, Treforest; 3rd George Cowdell, 17½ Yds, Tredegar; 4th W. C. Dawe, 17½ Yds, Tredegar.

Other results included a 150 Yards Whippet Race, won by Mr. Thomas's "Queen of Hearts" and Half Mile Handicap, won by L. Jakeman, Tongwynlais.

On the Monday evening after the heats of the Welsh Powderhall, a large crowd was still present to witness the Dirt Track Racing at 6.45 p.m. The "Holiday Handicap" was won by Y. Davies Other events were a "Flying Twelve Race" in which twelve scratch riders competed; an "August Handicap" and a "Holiday Scratch Race". Eric Peacock, the expert one-armed trick cyclist added a spice of variety and was much applauded.

In another meeting on August 10th 1929, Len Parker, Bristol, broke the track rolling start record. T. D. Lougher, the seventeen year old Pontypridd rider, who had leaped suddenly into prominence a few weeks before, figured in two exciting spills. Riding in the third heat of the Taff Handicap he collided with J. Thomas, Cardiff, who sustained an injury which prevented him from riding for the rest of the evening., while in the second heat of the Cynon Handicap, riding with his usual daring, came another cropper, but escaped unhurt. A large crowd was present.

World Champion At Taff Vale Park

Saturday, August 17th 1929 saw the first appearance at Taff Vale Park of "Sprouts" Elder, the worlds speedway champion. A record crowd saw the famous Nobbey Key, the clever Cardiff and Wembley rider, beat the standing start record held by Nick Carter, Brynmawr. Although "Sprouts" Elder, who had bad luck with his engine, did not perform quite as brilliantly as was expected, his visit resulted in the most thrilling and spectacular racing ever seen on the track. The first challenge race was a walk-over for Key, Elder's machine giving out, but the second race, from a rolling start, was a thrilling neck and neck affair from start to finish. Elder held the lead until the second lap, but Key passed him to beat him by two lengths. However, Elder gave an indication of his quality later, for in a Rolling Start Scratch Race he won easily. An Open Handicap Race with £5, £3 and £1 prizes, with 10/- to the winner of each of the four heats, was won by D. T. Morgan, Pontypridd. The following Saturday there was a £50 Challenge Race between Ron Baker, Merthyr and Len Parker, Bristol.

Another Rugby Return

In Late Summer 1929 the Pontypridd R.F.C. returned to play at Taff Vale Park. The Pontypridd Observer of 17th August 1929 gave this report: -

'For several years the rugby game has been played at Ynysangharad Park, but unfortunately the gates have been anything but satisfactory and the ground requires a rest, so the committee have turned their eyes in another direction and have secured the Taff Vale Park. In passing may I mention that Mr. Brooks, the pioneer and promoter of good sport in the town, has met the committee most generously. In

**Bryn Davies (Treforest), Welsh Powderhall
winner 1929 with trainer and backers**

the words of one "you cannot write anything too good about Mr. Brooks. He has proved a good samaritan." In a nutshell, rugby football will be played on the Taff Vale Park this year by a team that is going to bring honour, glory, and many visitors to the town. ' The rugby club failed to mention that the ground at Ynysangharad was unavailable because it had become overplayed and that the council had said that the field had to be relaid and rested.

Another New Sport On Taff Vale Park

On Thursday, September 15th 1929 to be exact, Pedal Cycle Racing on dirt track began, the first of its kind in Wales, under the control of Mr. J. E. Brooks, with over seventy competitors taking part. Mr. Brooks, however, had had troubles of his own that summer, and was prosecuted by the Inland Revenue. The Pontypridd Observer of 17th September 1929, gave the following story:-

Excise Prosecutions - T. V. Park Company Fined

A warning that if a similar case came before the bench again that the maximum penalty might be imposed, was given by the Stipendiary, Mr. D. Lleufer Thomas, M.A. at the Pontypridd police court on Wednesday, when three charges of admitting persons for payment and failing to comply with regulations for payment of entertainment duty, were brought against the Taff Vale Park Company Ltd; who were represented by the secretary, Mr. John Edward Brooks. Mr. David Gordon Hyslop, surveyor of customs and Excise stated that on June 22nd, 1929, an officer of customs and excise visited Taff Vale Park. He found that certain persons had paid for admission without receiving tickets. Entertainment duty was payable on all admissions exceeding 6d. Unless there was an arrangement for payment by certified returns, government stamps were issued.

The practice at the Taff Vale Park was for persons to be admitted through turnstiles. On this occasion Mr. Edmunds asked the defendant why there were no tickets and was given the explanation that the man responsible had gone for change. Under the finance act of 1916 the maximum penalty was £50 for each offence. Herbert Stanley Edmunds, the officer of Customs and Excise, said that he had visited Taff Vale Park on June 22nd. Some of the turnstiles were very busy. He disclosed his identity and watched for some minutes and saw one stile where no tickets were being issued. At the other turnstiles tickets were being issued in a regular manner. He spoke to the man taking the money at the stile where there were no tickets, and asked the reason. The man looked around and said "The man responsible is not here." Mr. Edmunds told the man that he should have stopped. The man said that no-one had gone through here, but Mr. Edmunds had seen about a dozen go through. Mr. Edmunds then found two men who had paid 2/4d each for themselves and a companion and had had no tickets.

Mr. Brooks suggested that they could not say definitely that the men came through the turnstile. Some people managed to sneak in. It was also difficult to get some people to take tickets. William Thomas Jones, Trehafod Road, Pontypridd, said that when the officer spoke to him that he had no ticket. He had not paid for admission as a complimentary ticket had been given him. Mr. Robert Tucker and Frank Morgan both spoke of paying for admission and not receiving a ticket. Mr. Brooks stated that 2,473 people had paid for admission that day. There was no intention to fraud. William Pitman, who gave evidence for the defence, said that he was giving out tickets at the stile. He left to get change, and told another man to watch the stile, but he misunderstood him.

The Stipendiary stated that the two cases where Morgan and Tucker had admitted the company would be fined £5, and the other case would be dismissed. The defendants were also ordered to pay 10/- costs, making a total of £10-10s.

Taff Vale Park Offered To Council

Dirt Track racing seems to have been J. E. Brooks' last throw of the dice as to making a profit out of Taff Vale Park, but could not have been a financial success for it did to re-appear for the summer of 1930 but sometime towards the end of 1929 it was offered to the

Pontypridd town council. The Pontypridd Observer of March 22nd 1930 carried the following report: -

'Some time ago Mr. J. E. Brooks, Pontypridd, offered the Taff Vale Park for sale to the Pontypridd Council. The matter was then referred to a sub-committee consisting of councillor J. Colenso Jones and Artemus Seymour. The council have decided to confirm the resolution put forward by this sub-committee: "That the council be recommended not to entertain the offer in view of the cost of the upkeep of the ground and the limited income likely to be obtained by the council in respect thereof." in other words "Not just yet."

The Greatest Zoo-Circus on Earth

On April 7th, 8th & 9th 1930, the residents of the Pontypridd district had the opportunity of seeing the Chapman's Great London Circus and Zoo at Taff Vale Park. The show was rated as probably the best that had toured Great Britain since Barnum and Bailey's. It included performing horses, and ponies, elephants, lions, polar bears, brown and black bears, man-eating tigers, leopards and numerous other birds, beasts and reptiles. The circus comprised of performances by some of the most talented artistes from the continental and English circuses.

Taff Vale Park - National Stadium?

The Glamorgan Free Press of May 3rd 1930 reported: *'After a rather lean time in the earlier stages of the season, Pontypridd RFC have settled down to a period of happiness and some prosperity. Pontypridd have the advantage of one of the finest grounds in South Wales at the Taff Vale Park, with excellent grandstand accommodation. In fact, when a proposal was recently put forward that a Welsh national ground should be provided, there were many that thought that such a good ground as the Taff Vale Park, situated in such a central town as Pontypridd would answer the purpose admirably. Negotiations are now on foot between the Pontypridd RFC committee and Mr. J. E. Brooks, the proprietor of the Taff Vale Park, to secure a long lease of the ground. Mr. Brooks is one of the keenest sportsmen in South Wales and is himself an old rugby player, who barely missed his international cap. He has been a most generous patron of all healthy sports for many decades, and has given great assistance to Pontypridd this season."*

Lord Lonsdale's Visit - Astonishing Reception

Notwithstanding the fact that a heavy cloud of depression hung over Pontypridd at the time (the end of May 1930), crowds of sports loving miners and their wives lined the streets to give a real Welsh welcome to Britain's chief sportsman. At the New Inn Hotel, Lord Lonsdale was received by Captain Arthur Seaton, Chairman of the council, who introduced him to Mr. Herbert R. Evans J.P; President of the Pontypridd organisation committee, and the members of the committee, and later was entertained to a luncheon by the Pontypridd Section of the Sports Charity commission.

After the luncheon they proceeded to the Taff Vale Park, where a mammoth sports day was already in progress. The fact that his lordship was there to present the trophies greatly enlarged the attendance and when he arrived at the park he was accorded a wonderful reception.

A splendid programme of events, consisting of a donkey derby, dirt track racing, whippet racing, by special request of Lord Lonsdale, under the Welsh Whippet Association, and Musical chairs on horseback was thoroughly enjoyed by Lord Lonsdale. Musical items were provided by the band of the 5th battalion of the Welch Regiment. When Lord Lonsdale presented some of the trophies it was found that there was a £5 note inside one of the cups. The recipient of this cup thought there was some mistake, but his lordship informed him that the money was his and it would be more useful than a cup. Later, after being entertained to tea at the New Inn Hotel, Lord Lonsdale proceeded to the Common, where he laid a wreath at the war memorial. He also visited the Rocking Stone before proceeding to Cardiff. This event raised £156, £25 of which was donated by Lord Lonsdale.

It is difficult to say what was happening at Taff Vale Park during the summer of 1930, the above event was a highlight, but the Pontypridd

**Les Thomas (Treforest), Welsh Powderhall
winner 1930 with brother and trainer Illtyd Thomas**

Observer of August 2nd intimated that there were weekly sports as well and wrote: - Taff Vale Weekly Sports - *There was a good attendance on Monday evening at the Taff Vale Park sports organised by Mr. Danny Davies, of Cardiff. Handicapper, Mr. John Doran, Queen Adelaide Hotel, Treforest. Entertaining sports were greyhound, whippet, and foot racing which were the chief features.'*

The 1930 Welsh Powderhall - The last Meeting

This would turn out to be the final year of this event. Teddy Lewis had given up on Taff Vale Park, and ran a rival ' Welsh Powderhall ' the same weekend at Virginia Park, Caerphilly. The attendance the first day of the Welsh Powderhall meeting held at the Taff Vale Park on Saturday and Monday, August 28th and 30th, 1930, was noticeably small. This year's event did not attract more than one hundred entries for the £100 prize for the 130 Yards Race. The attendance on Monday was much better and the sport generally keener. Two wing-threequarters of the Pontypridd RFC ran first and second in the final of the Powderhall sprint. They were Les Thomas, Treforest, the winner, who won in 12 seconds off 12½ Yds, and Selwyn Fletcher, Treforest, 16½ Yds, who was second. The other finalists were G. E. Evans, 17½ Yds, Abercynon, and F. J. Cunwood, 17½ Yds, Abercynon.

Thomas won after one of the most spirited contests seen in the finals of the Powderhall for some years. He got off his mark well, overtook Evans halfway and breasted the tape with half a yard to spare over Fletcher. Inches divided Fletcher and Evans, Cunwood being fourth. Thomas was second in last year's Powderhall and third in 1927. He was also successful in winning a £15 Handicap at Tonypandy in 1927. Other events were: 60 Yards Boys Race; 500 Yards Greyhound Race; and 120 Yards Whippet Race.

5th Battalion Inspection

On a Sunday in Oct 1930 Field Marshal Viscount Allenby visited Pontypridd to inspect the 5th Battalion of the Welch Regiment of which he was Honorary Colonel. A large crowd watched the review which took place at Taff Vale Park. In the course of his speech he said that he had no idea so many men in the ranks would be able to wear war medals. He later inspected a large number of the members of the battalion who paraded under the command of Colonel Phillips. In a short speech after the parade Viscount Allenby said that the men of the 5th Welch had helped mould victory in the campaign in Palestine. A reception was afterwards held at the Drill Hall, where he expressed the hope that the country would not have to go through another war. The effort had been terrible, but he was confident that should war be thrust upon this country again, the courage of this land would carry us through to victory.

Taff Vale Park Up For Sale

At a meeting of the Pontypridd Urban District Council Education Committee on October 28th 1930, a letter from Mr. A. S. John, Accountant, Pontypridd, was read, stating that it had come to his notice that the committee were anxious to acquire the Taff Vale Park for the purpose of playing fields for school children and that as he was interested in the matter, he was authorized to state, on behalf of his clients, that they would be prepared to meet the committee in a reasonable spirit. It was decided that a sub - committee, consisting of the members of the Treforest Ward, together with the chairman, be instructed to consider and report upon the matter.

Offer of Purchase of Taff Vale Park

At another Education Committee meeting on November 25th 1930 it was reported that Councillor John Jones had inspected the Taff Vale Park on November 4th, and that councillors D. L. Davies J. P; J. Howell, J. Jones, G. J. Maddocks and R. Roper J. P.; had inspected the same on November 24th 1930. It was stated that the area of land was six acres and two roots, or thereabouts, and that the whole of the land including the stand erected thereon had been offered to the education committee for the sum of £2,500. The sub - committee recommended that they be given plenary power to negotiate for the purchase of the freehold at the figure of £2,000, but not exceeding £2,500, subject to the approval of the Government Departments concerned. It was further reported by the secretary that H.M. Inspector of Schools had informed him that the Board of Education were prepared to give favourable consideration to the proposal if this committee could come to reasonable terms with the vendor and that such proposal, if approved, would rank for grant at 50%. The secretary intimated that he had been informed by the vendor's agent that £2,500 was the lowest figure which could be considered for the sale of the park.

Acquisition of Taff Vale Park by Council

At the next Education Committee meeting on December 17th 1930, the secretary reported that since the last meeting he had been in communication with the district valuer with a view to an official valuation being placed on the Taff Vale Park, and the report of the valuer dated December 13th, was favourable. He further reported having communicated with the Board of Education thereon on December 15th, enclosing plans, and stressing the importance of an early decision being reached with regards to the proposal. On January 27th, the secretary reported having asked the clerk of the council on December 24th 1930 to sign Board of Education form 349G, in triplicate, in connection with the Taff Vale Park, and same was submitted to the Board on December 31st 1930.

A communication from the Board of Education to the Pontypridd Education Committee, dated January 6th 1931, approved the plans for the purpose of the playing field, and stated they were prepared to sanction the expenditure of £2,600 involved, subject to the approval of the proper loan by the Ministry of health. The board assumed that in view of the nature of the use of the ground at present, very little expenditure would be necessary for its adaptation for playing field purposes. The board asked for the submission of plans of the grandstand and dressing room, etc; and the secretary reported that he had issued instructions accordingly. The secretary reported having notified the clerk of the council of the boards approval and that the clerk, in a memorandum dated January 7th 1931, had informed him that a council meeting on January 6th 1931, had passed a resolution authorizing an application to the Ministry of Health for sanction to borrow the sum of £2,600. In view of the uncertainty as to whether the sanction of the Ministry of Health would be obtained, it was resolved - that the chairman and secretary be authorized to take what steps they deemed advisable in the matter and if necessary invoke the aid of the Member of Parliament in connection therewith. At a later stage in the meeting a letter was read from Messrs. Chapman and Co. intimating that they intended visiting Pontypridd again this year with their travelling zoo, and asking if the Taff Vale Park would be available. The director, Mr. D. Milton Jones, intimated that if the land was in their hand by that time it would not be advisable to let it for that purpose as so much damage would be caused. One of the members remarked that the ground could not be more damaged more than it was at present. There was far too much football being played there, and if this was continued there would not be a blade of grass to be seen on the ground.

Grandstand Damaged

At a meeting of the education sub-committee on February 4th 1931, the secretary reported that he had received the sanctions of the Ministry of Health for the acquisition of the Taff Vale Park, and this necessitated prompt action. The secretary reported that he had decided to convene a meeting of the sub-committee immediately, in consequence of the damage which occurred to a portion of the grand stand on the Taff Vale Park early on the morning of Sunday, February 1st, 1931. He stated that we have inspected the grandstand and have instructed the surveyor to have same thoroughly examined and report the probable cost of making it secure.

At another sub-committee meeting on march 24th 1931, the secretary reported correspondence with the clerk of the council with reference to completion of the purchase of the Taff Vale Park and having arranged, in view of the fact that the estimates for the current financial year made no provision for any expenditure in connection therein, that such completion be effected on April 1st 1931, to which all parties had agreed. A memorandum dated March 24th 1931, was received from the clerk of the council, enclosing a copy of the completion account in connection with the sale of the Taff Vale Park as follows: - Purchase Price - £2,500, less agreed rates to March 31st 1931, - £25. Balance Due - £2,475. The clerk of the council suggested that cheques be drawn in favour of Messrs Morgan and Roberts, solicitors, for the vendors, for the sum of £2,475 and for the council for the sum of £25, the agreed deduction from the purchase price on account of rates due to the council. In addition, the clerk stated that it would be necessary to draw cheques in respect of stamp duties, search fees, and preparation of plans, particulars relating to which would be supplied in due course.

At the end of March 1931 the final of "The Glamorgan Times Cup" of the Pontypridd Sunday Football League was played at the Taff Vale Park, and went to another replay a week later.

Education Committee Meeting April 22nd 1931

Prior to a special meeting of the education committee and the Park Boys' Council School on April 22nd 1931 the members inspected the Taff Vale Park, which had recently been acquired for educational purposes. The secretary reported having received several applications for the use of the Park, some of which he had refused outright, whilst others had practically been arranged before the conveyance of the site to the education authority. He also reported that an application had been received for the hire of the park during next season by the Pontypridd Rugby Club. After mature consideration, it was resolved, on the motion of councillor John Howell, seconded by Councillor Dan Evans: That inasmuch as the Taff Vale Park has been acquired for educational purposes that the practice of hiring it for sports and other functions be discontinued, with the exception of civic functions, when it can be used with the sanction of the education committee from time to time.

The secretary was authorized to sanction the use of the park for outstanding football matches which had been arranged during April and May, on the distinct understanding that persons having the use of the Park must indemnify the authority in respect of any liability which may accrue through the defective state of the stand.

The state of the grandstand was considered and a memorandum from the surveyor, dated February 11th, 1931, was read, in which he suggested that, without going thoroughly into the details, a new roof should be placed over a portion of the stand only, and that the back five rows of the stand should be removed and some of the seats made use of in the front of the stand, which would make the front safer and would keep the stand building about 11 or 12 feet further away from the school, thereby improving the light. The surveyor stated further that the roof should be a light steel one constructed with a fall towards the playing field, instead of towards the school, and that the estimated cost of these works would be £600 to £700.

The secretary having reported that there was no provision in the estimate for such expenditure, it was resolved, on the motion of Councillor David Williams, second by Councillor R. Roper, J.P; - that the surveyor cause the roof to be removed, and anything likely to cause danger through falling, and the material thus removed be utilized by the groundsman for strengthening the fencing on the ground. David Williams stressed the importance of the strictest supervision being maintained when the children were at the park so as to avoid them falling into the river when playing on that side. It was resolved - That notices warning trespassers on the Park should be posted.

League Championship Decider

On Friday, May 1st 1931, the Glamorgan League Championship Rugby Play-off match was played between Mountain Ash and Treorchy at Taff Vale Park before a large crowd of between 3 and 4,000. Even after 15 minutes each extra-time, there was still no score, and the match was replayed the following season at Ynysangharad Park.

Didn't Rugby Club Bid For Taff Vale Park?

With the Pontypridd Urban District Council now owning Taff Vale Park, the local rugby club's short but successful spell there came to an end. At the annual meeting of the Pontypridd R.F.C. held at the White Hart Hotel on Tuesday evening, June 23rd 1931, the chairman, Supt. J. L. Rees, M.B.E. in the course of his address said that they were losing the use of the Taff Vale Park which had been the scene of many memorable conflicts during the past two seasons.

They were going back to their old ground, the Ynysangharad Park, and they intended approaching the Welsh Rugby Union for a grant to enable them to erect dressing rooms on the ground. With the Pontypridd Rugby Club playing at Taff Vale Park while it was up for sale, one would think that they would have thought about buying it, but at the time nothing appeared in the local newspapers, and it was not until a report of the club's Annual General Meeting at the White Hart Hotel in June 1932 that this question was answered. And yes, it appears that the rugby club DID want the Taff Vale Park. The club secretary, Mr. Harold Roberts stated:-

"At the last general meeting the question arose regarding the acquisition of the Taff Vale Park as a playing ground, and some few weeks later I received a letter from the Welsh Rugby Union stating that the price asked for the ground was prohibitive. The opportunity was lost, only to be readily settled by another body. But maybe that is not the whole story", continued the secretary in a very straightforward mode of speech, *"shortly afterwards, the union purchased a ground elsewhere, so that it appears that the negotiations were proceeding even while the acquisition of the Taff Vale Park was under consideration. Did the Union seriously consider the purchase of the Taff Vale Ground, or were the visits paid to inspect it and the meetings that were held with the Pontypridd officials merely arranged to gild the pill?"*

Scouts At Taff Vale Park

On August 29th 1931 there was a garden fete held at Taff Vale Park for all the local scout troops. Madame Muriel Jones and her Royal Ladies Choir gave renditions throughout the afternoon. Mr. Chiefly gave trips around the park in a motor-cycle combination.

Mammoth Sports Festival At Pontypridd

Colossal is probably the most apt qualification that can be applied to the First Annual Sports of the Pontypridd Urban District Council Schools held at the Taff Vale Park on Friday September 18th 1931. Organised on an immense scale, the festival was in many respects unique. Some idea of the vastness of the event may be gauged from the fact that more than 2,000 pupils took part. The lighter vein of carnivalia was represented by a Novel Fancy Dress Competition, and the interest sustained by the various items made one forget the ominous appearance of the low-flying clouds which hung overhead.

Review

The late 1920s had seen new and exciting sports at the Taff Vale Park, with John Edward Brooks trying to make the ground a viable proposition. Dirt track and greyhound racing had kept the place just ticking over, but a lot of money was not being made. The Welsh Powderhall was declining and compared to the past the crowds were now small, and the competitors local, rather than international. J. E. Brooks had increased his charge to Teddy Lewis and his associates to such an extent that the 1930 Welsh Powderhall was the last, and was moved to Caerphilly. Perhaps the prosecution by the tax people was the last straw for J. E. Brooks, for as the lease for greyhound racing came to an end he had offered the ground to the local education authority.

For the last forty years Taff Vale Park had been the centre of sport in Pontypridd and the surrounding district, crowds of many thousands, sometimes reportedly between 20,000 and 40,000 (A slight exaggeration I think!) had been present for some of the Welsh Powderhall meetings. Large crowds had been seen for the Rugby League internationals, while the Pontypridd Rugby League and Dragons soccer team had often had crowds of two or three thousand, and often more. By the late 1920s the public had become bored with athletics and cycling, and this also contributed to the decline of Taff Vale Park. Of course, the economic situation had not helped. The miners were poorly paid and sometimes on strike, and the whole country was in an industrial depression, and people did not have the money to spend on entertainments when they were struggling to feed their families.

By the summer of 1930 the speedway and greyhound racing had disappeared, probably because they were not making a profit, and the contracts were not renewed. 1931 saw a new era in the history of Taff Vale Park with its purchase by the Pontypridd Urban District

Council. A Pontypridd Schools Athletic Association was soon set up and it appeared that Taff Vale Park was now out of reach of the general public and would be used for the sole use of the children of the local schools. However, the education authority soon found that the upkeep of Taff Vale Park was a heavy financial burden, and after many arguments it was agreed that if it did not interfere with the schools using the ground, Taff Vale Park could be rented out for events that would first have to be vetted by the authority. Indirectly, the authority had opened up Taff Vale Park for local organisations, and a new golden era of carnivals and fetes was about to begin, and it would appear that the famous Taff Vale Park was again reborn.

Chapter 8

The Three Wise men

The names of Teddy Lewis, David Williams, and John Edward Brooks are synonymous with Taff Vale Park. These are their stories

Teddy Lewis

Mr. Tom Edward Lewis was the youngest of five children, born to Mr. Tom Lewis, who was a boot and shoe manufacturer and owned a shop in Taff Street, Pontypridd, and was born on a farm between Church Village and Llantwit Fardre. His family later moved to Pontypridd, and as a youngster Ted was a great swimmer, and used to dive off the Berw Bridge into the River Taff at the famous Berw Pool. He grew up to become the "Mr. Sportsman" of the town of Pontypridd, and was influential in the Pontypridd Rugby Club, either as an advisor or an administrator, and was president of the club in seasons 1911-12, '12-13, '13-14, and patron 1919-20 + '20-21. Teddy was Vice-president of the Welsh Rugby Union for ten years, he held the position of secretary of the Glamorgan Rugby league for twenty-two years, and was president of the Pontypridd cricket club.

T. E. Lewis was educated at Clifton College, Bristol, and after leaving school he went to sea. After an adventurous period of gun-running during the South American Civil War when he was shipwrecked for weeks when on a banana boat, Teddy returned to Pontypridd, but never ate a banana for the rest of his life! From the earliest days at school, however, it was sport that attracted him, and his administrative activities, business acumen and conscientious adherence to principles made him popular. He abhorred coursing and any sort of sport where "both sides did not have an equal chance" but there were few sports in which he did not play an active part. As a manager of boxers, handicapper in pedestrianism, and rugby football administrator, he was considered to be incomparable, but always served his native country first.

He was a respected official and a delightful after-dinner speaker who was often in great demand, and even when not on the Pontypridd Rugby Club committee, whenever they ran into problems that they could not handle themselves, it was always Teddy Lewis that they turned to. However, it is in connection with Taff Vale Park, and the Welsh Powderhall that everyone, even today, remember his name with affection. When Taff Vale Park came up for sale in 1900, Teddy became the secretary of the Athletic Syndicate that leased the park. It was he who probably suggested a Welsh Powderhall, and he fired the starting pistol in every Powderhall for the 27 years of its promotion until 1932. He was the official starter for the South Wales Athletics Board, and no important meeting was complete without Ted and his famous starting pistols, which would often startle unwary people with their loud bang. In all, Teddy used four pistols, three of which were mid 19th century muzzle loading, using black powder and pad, fired by a percussion cap, while the fourth was a late 19th century sporting pistol possibly of European manufacture. The 'Blunderbuss' was used mainly to start the longer Powderhall races, and it was reported that once in a mile race a man on scratch was hit on the backside by the pad from the gun, obtaining a flying start! A cartoon of this event was drawn by J. C. Walker of the Western Mail.

In 1930 Teddy Lewis, along with Tom Coggins, decided to move the Welsh Powderhall to Caerphilly. Teddy stated that ' serious financial losses' had been incurred by keeping it at Pontypridd, and although he was Pontypridd born and bred, sentiment alone could not see the continuation of the race at Taff Vale Park. Other athletic events were charged £20 for the hire of the stadium compared to the £75 charged to the Welsh Powderhall promoters.

Boxing was one of his great loves, he was a talented trainer, and organised boxing matches called "Assaults at Arms" and annual athletic meetings in aid of the rugby club. He became manager of the Millfield Boxing Club, who staged boxing nights at the booth at the People's Park, Mill Street, and took on a young boxer called Jimmy Wilde, who under Teddy Lewis's guidance, would become a boxing legend, and was soon seven stone champion of Wales, British Champion, and a Lonsdale belt holder, and was unlucky to lose an 8 stone world championship fight. In his 1938 autobiography Jimmy Wilde wrote:

"I shall never forget how Teddy Lewis looked that first night. Short, with grey hair white afterwards turned pure white; a very fresh pink and white skin, and a pair of pince-nez that made him look more like a schoolmaster than a boxing club manager. He was a little deaf, even at that time, and later grew stone deaf. It is impossible to estimate the value of Ted's help, patience and advice, and what is more remarkable is that at the beginning he did it for nothing. Yes, Ted was always cool, detached and methodical, and forced me to take on at least one of his habits, always looking after the job in hand."

Ted's silver hair was famous in the boxing world, almost as famous as his reputation, for once Ted gave his word, he always kept it, and that is why Jimmy Wilde seldom fought under contract. When he launched his famous trio of Percy Jones, Jimmy Wilde, and Llew Edwards, on the boxing world he was imbued with the idea of carrying on the traditions established by the late Tom Thomas, Fred Welsh and Jim Driscoll. Jones, Wilde and Edwards won Lonsdale Belts, and Mr. Lewis definitely established a niche in the history of the National Sporting Club with the "Welsh Night". When Frank Moody won the British Cruiser-weight title in 1928 it was the fourth Lonsdale Belt brought through Ted Lewis. He managed the boxing affairs of Jimmy Wilde until he retired after the defeat by Pancho Villa. The purse paid to Wilde - £13,000 - was a record for a fly-weight championship of the world, and Mr. Lewis made boxing history when he arranged that Mrs. Wilde should receive £5,000 of this sum for "allowing her husband to box!"

He also held vice-presidencies of the Pontypridd Swimming Club, County Football Club, Pontypridd Kennel Club, and the Welsh Amateur Boxing Association, and was a generous supporter of the Glamorgan County Cricket Club. Teddy Lewis' main residences in Pontypridd were in Penuel Lane opposite the market entrance, now used by James the Greengrocers, and in Lan Park Road, at No. 2 and later at Dan-y-coed. He spent his last days at Hillside, Lan Park Road, and died, aged 70, at his sons (Ted Junior) home on Monday, 17th April, 1933 having had a seizure on the previous Wednesday. He is buried in an unmarked grave at Glyntaff Cemetery.

One national newspaper wrote at the time of his death:

'Wherever sportsmen gathered this week expressions of regret at the death of Teddy Lewis, Pontypridd, have been heard. He was more than a sportsman to them; he was a "character" as outstanding as could be possibly imagined. The trick he manoeuvred to prevent a gang of toughs getting their hands on some of Jimmy Wilde's purse money at once gives insight to his shrewdness and resource.

Coming away from Olympia, Teddy had with him £2,000 in six banknotes - part of the purse. He was followed by the "gang", who booked rooms adjoining his own in the hotel. He knew from the experience of friends how formidable they were, and he was in despair about the cash. Before retiring he took the daring step of placing the banknotes in his shoes before depositing them outside his bedroom door. Shortly after midnight the gang entered and ransacked every corner of the room. Happily they left "Teddy" alone, but he lay with fear and trembling underneath his clothes. Finally they left.'

John Edward Brooks

John Edward Brooks was the last private owner of Taff Vale Park, and his story is a very interesting one. His father and vivacious Irish wife moved from Wolverhampton to Park Street, Treforest in 1875, where they opened a gentlemen's hairdressing salon and tobacconist business. Later there was a shop on the site of the present Cafe Royal, and finally the family moved to new premises at 88 Taff Street. The younger sons would get work in the Newbridge Chainworks, but John followed in the family business and became a hairdresser and when his father Isiah Brooks died, as the eldest son the business passed into his hands and he became a most successful businessman, and as a tobacco wholesaler supplied all the shops in the Rhondda Valleys.

As a young boy, he played rugby football for Pontypridd, and in 1881 he was selected to play for Wales, but unfortunately, the Welsh selectors forgot to tell him! The game was the first ever Welsh international rugby match, and he was never selected again. J. E. Brooks once said:

John Edward Brooks (with Fish) last private owner of Taff Vale Park

'There was no organisation or committee assisting in 1880 to select players. All that would happen was that some individual would have a conversation with you, take your name and address, and pass it on. That happened to me after I had played for Pontypridd against Shewbooks School at Sophia Gardens, Cardiff. It was mentioned to me that Edward Treharne and I had been chosen to play for Wales against England in that first international. I had no definite instructions from anyone to play in that match. But I heard afterwards that I had been expected to play.'

He was a founder member of the Pontypridd Fire Brigade and spent 21 years on the force, and was a staunch Catholic. Around 1918 he apparently went on a hunting trip and a gash on his leg somehow got infected and ended in him having his leg amputated. He became a wealthy man and lived in one of the large houses on the Parade, Trallwn, but eventually moved to Porthcawl.

The whole Brooks family has always been well-known in local sporting circles, and J. E. Brooks was the first President of the Welsh Boxing Board of control. After the shop had closed for the evening, his three sons and their friends would go down to the basement, where there was a 12 foot boxing ring. J. E. Brooks was "fishing mad", and won the "News of the World" fishing rod one year for the biggest catch of the season. A boat was kept by the family, and if he knew there was a shoal of whiting coming up the channel, he and his sons would b e out there in a flash.

Interviewed in January 2000 John Phillip Brooks, grandson of J. E. Brooks, remembered that his grandfather was a 'hard' man who insisted that things were done properly. If people were supposed to chew meat 28 times, then he kept an eye on his family during meals to ensure that this was indeed carried out. John Edward apparently ruled his family like he ruled his business, with a firm hand. Those were the days when Woodbines were five for 1d, and a good pipe could be bought for 6d. and work in the barber's shop sometimes went on until 1 a.m. John Philip seems to contradict the above report about the loss of his grandfathers leg, and insists that he lost his leg after a fire near the White Palace Cinema when he was a fireman, when broken timber had fallen down on him and an injury to his leg turned gangrenous and eventually necessitated its removal. His grandfather did not walk with a limp, but rather as if he had a stiff leg. He also recalls staying in Porthcawl and going out fishing with his grandfather, who was not averse to staying out longer than he had told his wife he would be. He remembers that every morning his grandfather would go out swimming between 6 & 7 a.m. in the stone swimming pool on the beach near the pier, and if his children and grandchildren were not out of bed before he returned home, he would hit them with his wet towel until they got up. Asked why did he think his grandfather had not been informed that he had been selected for Wales and why the other Pontypridd player, Edward Treharne, had not mentioned it, he replied that the fact that John Edward Brooks was a working man, rather than the high or middle class youths that were playing rugby at the time, might have been a cause, but whether this was a deliberate mistake or not he was not sure. Also, the Pontypridd club, whose other players were training to be solicitors etc, did not play that often in 1881, and it is possible that John Edward Brooks and Edward Treharne had never even met each other let alone played together.

In the 1920s he was a shareholder and secretary of 'the Dragons' the professional soccer team that was playing at Taff Vale Park. It was reported in the Pontypridd Observer in 1922 that he would travel up fro Porthcawl to watch every Dragons football match. He was elected chairman of the new Pontypridd rugby league team in August 1926, and when that folded he bought the shares off the other directors and became sole owner of Taff Vale Park. He promoted dirt track racing and greyhound racing for nearly four years, but in 1930 offered Taff Vale Park to the local council. The following year he sold it to the Pontypridd Urban District Council. This indomitable old sportsman, however, lived on until the Second World War, and died at the ripe old age of 85 on November 17th 1944, and was buried at Glyntaff Cemetery. He was a close friend of the famous boxer Frank Moody. J. E. Brooks and Sons, the tobacconists, of 88 Taff Street closed for the final time on June 30th 1959 and the premises were converted by Lipton's into one of their multiple grocery stores.

David Williams

David Williams was a native of Quakers Yard, and was the son of the late Thomas Williams and the late Amelia Pritchard. For 21 years he was a member of the Pontypridd Urban District Council, of which he was chairman on two occasions, and he was for six years a member of the Glamorgan County Council. When the Pontypridd and Rhondda Joint Water Board took over the old Pontypridd Water Works Board, he was the first chairman of the Joint Board, of which he was chairman during many subsequent years. He was a founder member and chairman of the Taff Fechan Water Board.

In the realm of athletic sports his name was a household word in South Wales. As chairman and organiser of the Pontypridd Athletic Club he was practically responsible (wrote the Pontypridd Observer) for the construction of the Taff Vale Park, the famous sportsground at which the Welsh Powderhall and many other important athletic and cycling events were held for many years and helped turn it into one of the finest athletic stadiums in the country. He was the first chairman of the Pontypridd professional soccer club (the Dragons) and for many years was a member of the executive of the Welsh Football Association, and a keen support and sometime committee man of the Pontypridd R.F.C. He was official timekeeper for the British Empire Championship held in London and famous boxing champions used to appear at the many boxing tournaments he promoted at the Pontypridd Town Hall in aid of Nazareth House, Cardiff. On Sunday Oct 18th 1937 David Williams, for 52 years the licensee of the Greyhound Hotel, which was the headquarters of the Welsh Powderhall, passed away at the age of 76.

James Roberts J.P.

Without James Roberts there would never have been a Taff Vale Park. James Roberts was born at Heol Marck Farm, Cowbridge, in 1835, his parents came to Pontypridd in 1838. After school years, in 1850 he went to Mountain Ash as a grocer, and then in 1855 to Aberdare as a junior hand at the shop in connection with the Abernant Works. In 1863 he married the grand-daughter of Mr. Lewis, The Boot, Aberdare. In 1869 he became manager of the

Llwncoed blast furnaces, and in 1878 the manager of the Forest Iron and Steel Work's Co. at Treforest until they closed fourteen years later. James Roberts lived at Taff House, Treforest. He became a member of the Glamorgan County Council, Chairman of the Pontypridd burial Board and the County School of governors and various other committee's. He always associated himself energetically with the political, social, religious movements in the district. Throughout his life he was an ardent advocate for the best educational facilities for the people, and always tried to impress upon the young the need for them to make best use of their school years. If he had a hobby it may be said that it was working for the education of the children. In 1890 he allowed the re-constituted Pontypridd Football Club to rent his company's land in Treforest so that they could build a stadium that would later become known as Taff Vale Park. James Roberts was President of Pontypridd RFC in seasons 1890-91, 91-92, and 93-94. He was probably the owner of Taff Vale Park until his death age 82 on March 1st 1917. Owing to ill-health, he had for some time been unable to attend the meetings of the bodies of which he was still the chairman, viz; the burial board and the county school board of governors.

James Roberts J.P.

BIBLIOGRAPHY

Tries In The Valleys - London League Publications 1998.
The Great Welsh Spirit - Pub. Gwyn Thomas 1999
Pontypridd R.F.C. at Taff Vale Park - Coalopolis Publications 1999.
The Butchers Arms Boys - Pontypridd R.F.C. - The Early Years - Pub. Rugby Unlimited 1997.
Fields of Praise - W.R.U. Official History.
The Glamorgan County Times - Pontypridd Observer - South Wales Daily News - Western Mail -South Wales Echo - Sports Echo.

Author at T.V. Park February 2000